Motherhood and God

Motherhood and God

MARGARET HEBBLETHWAITE

GEOFFREY CHAPMAN
LONDON

A Geoffrey Chapman book published by
Cassell Ltd
1 Vincent Square, London SW1P 2PN

First published 1984

ISBN 0 225 66384 8

British Library Cataloguing in Publication Data

Hebblethwaite, Margaret
    Motherhood and God.
    1. Mothers
    I. Title
    261.8'358743   HQ759

Printed in Great Britain by
Fletcher & Son Ltd, Norwich

*For Dominic,
Cordelia
and Benedict*

Among the several people who in various ways
have helped this book to be born, a special
acknowledgement is due to Dominic Maruca SJ
of the Gregorian University in Rome. He first set
me off in this direction, brought to my notice the
passage from T. S. Eliot, and encouraged me to
produce something for publication, little
thinking that it would turn out to be not an
article but an entire book.

Contents

We had the experience but missed the meaning,
And approach to the meaning restores the
   experience
In a different form, beyond any meaning
We can assign to happiness. I have said before
That the past experience revived in the meaning
Is not the experience of one life only
But of many generations . . . .

T. S. Eliot, *The Dry Salvages*, II

Introduction

This book is about finding God in motherhood, and finding motherhood in God.

I believe there is only one starting point for such a project, and that is human experience. The experience I write of is my own experience, as a mother of three small children, and I write of deep and churning emotions, as well as of the frustrating material details of everyday life. I have tried to evoke a sense of what it feels like to be a mother, but I do not want to stop there. I want to show how God can bring meaning to the experience, and the experience can bring meaning to God.

I say this to explain why this book does not fit the usual categories. Those who are interested in reading about having babies do not expect to turn the page and find themselves up against a lot of holy talk. Those who are interested in reading about God do not expect to have to wade through a heap of dirty nappies to get there. But to keep life and religion apart in such a way is false to both sides. More and more persistently, theologians throughout the world are calling for an experience-based theology. They know that if faith does not spring out of and return to the ground soil of daily existence, then it means nothing. Faith needs life to find its true nature.

At the same time life needs faith. The strong emotions aroused by motherhood and the everyday slog of bringing up children find their true meaning as part of a relationship with God. I have tried in this book to make motherhood at the same time more real and more Christian; I have tried to write about this very common experience in a way that will make the reader say at the same time 'yes, that's it', and 'oh, so that's what it is'; I have tried to show how God is the answer to all our searchings even here, in our motherhood, where we have not yet deeply sought her.

'Her' is the obvious way to speak of the God we find in motherhood — the God who is not only our father but also our mother. And yet it comes as a shock, and it is only when we have fully accustomed ourselves to the change of language that we can begin to respond to the new associations. It is worth making that effort, because there are new levels of response in us that can be awakened by thinking of God as female. I have no doubt that this move is legitimate, and I also believe it has traditional roots — there is more on this in Chapter 16. But it is more than just legitimate and traditional, it is also becoming increasingly urgent: more and more people are asking to escape from the limitations of an exclusively male-orientated view of God, though without quite knowing how to go about it, or what to say next after 'God is she . . .'.

As I have tried to find those next things to say, I have let the book fall into two sections. Part One talks of the experience of motherhood, largely through my own story, and explores what our own maternal caring can tell us of God's love. Part Two concentrates on some practical ways in which a mother can nourish her faith: it is difficult for her to find space and opportunity for prayer, for the sacraments and for theology, and yet she has valuable insights to bring if only she can find the right opening.

But before plunging into my experience of mothering I look back at my experience of being mothered — at my childhood and adolescence. Showing where I have come from sheds light on where I am going. Here is where I began to learn about motherhood, and began to learn about God.

1

Prelude:
being mothered

I have only hazy memories of what my mother told me about God. I know that she did speak on the subject, because I retain a strong impression that my earliest religious education — and so ultimately the most author-itative — came from my two parents. I seem to remember that when my mother tucked me into bed each night and turned out the light she would always say 'God bless', and that sometimes she would perhaps spell out more explicitly that God would look after me through the night because he loved me and I was his child. Any sense I have of God's cherishing, protecting love must derive from the fact that my cherishing, protecting mother mediated this belief: she reminded me of it each night, expressing it in her own words, and suggesting that it was bigger, softer, surer and more long-lasting than anything she could offer.

God, of course, was not spoken of as our mother, but as our father. It was the Church, or Mary, that was our mother. I have come to regret this division of genders, and this book is an attempt to find what truth there is in calling God our mother, to meditate on what human motherhood can tell us about God's love.

Despite the terminological problem, I did learn to associate maternal qualities with God. My earliest mass book had a picture of a big woman holding out her cloak for lots of people to shelter under. Probably the image was meant in the first place to be the Church, or Our Lady, but it was naturally associated with the way God looked after us and gathered us together. Another early prayer book I had, *For the Smallest Person*, had a wonderful assortment of family imagery. Baby Jesus is shown as a playmate, or a little brother; guardian angels lead us by the hand, pour out bathwater for us (in an old-fashioned tin tub), or tidy our clothes; Jesus appears again looking slightly older, blessing and supervising the children washing up; his house, the Church, is a home also for us, as two angels hold wide open the doors, and another two lead us by the skirt; Mummy and Daddy are put in relationship to God as we stand in relationship to them: 'Take care of them, because they take care of me. Give them all they need, because they give me my dinner, my clothes, and my toys and all I need.' This first prayer book, that made a great impression on me when I was small, is now lovingly preserved for my own children, much torn, much drawn on, and with strips of browny-yellow sticky tape holding each page to the next.

It came as a nasty shock to me when my elder brother explained to me about the age of six that Mummy was not a Catholic. I had only recently learned to distinguish in meaning between Christian and Catholic, but I had naturally presumed that we were all on the right side together, especially as I had noticed no difference between the teaching of my two parents. Perhaps it was because of that blow at authority that I lost precise recollections of my mother's religious teaching, or perhaps it is simply because it was so far back. Up till that time, Mummy's church and Daddy's church had been like Mummy's bank and Daddy's bank. We used to go to the Anglicans for Harvest Festival at least. My brother, however, was taught at school that it was wrong to worship in Protestant churches, and so the practice had to stop. What a cruel insult to my parents' marriage that now seems.

My parents remained sufficiently liberal and daring to send me to an Anglican primary school, because they thought it was better as well as closer than the Catholic alternative. But from the age of eleven my father was firm that I should go to a convent to receive a proper Catholic education.

When I went to the convent school I already knew a fair amount about my faith. I knew that Catholics were right and Protestants wrong, and that this was demonstrated by the added seriousness with which Catholics practised their faith. Protestants merely went to church when they felt like it, and even then did not genuflect or use holy water. Even when they were supposed to be kneeling down they rested their bottoms on the bench behind. They excused themselves from going to confession on the grounds that they confessed to God in their hearts, when I knew as well as anyone else that this meant they did nothing at all. To excuse themselves from the inconvenience of serious Christian practice they invented lies about Catholics that they kept on repeating without attending to the explanations that we Catholics were always ready to give. They said we worshipped statues. As for them, they hardly even worshipped God, since they did not believe in the Real Presence. Even if they pretended to they clearly did not, as they did not keep the Sacrament reserved as we did with a red sanctuary lamp. A Protestant church was just empty. I felt sorry for my Protestant friends, and was glad when there was a chance to pray for the conversion of England.

At my convent school I was to imbibe much more about what God liked and was like. Our first form mistress was a nun called Mother B. Mother B was kind but strict, and she always wore a big smile. One day one of the girls asked her why she was always smiling. She looked pleased as punch that this had been remarked upon, but would not say. One day I came across her suddenly in a corridor after school hours when she thought she was alone. She was not smiling, in fact she looked rather sad, and I almost failed to recognize her until she saw there was someone there and smiled. Usually she was very careful to keep smiling if there was a chance anyone might be watching her, such as when she was crossing the playground.

Mother B was not impressed that I had been in a missionary situation in a Protestant school. She was a little alarmed that I was the only girl in the form not to have been confirmed, my more free-thinking parents having decided, after discussion with the parish priest, that seven was too young an age for this sacrament. The omission was rapidly put right. Then she was extremely dubious about the level of Catholic education I had so far received, despite weekly classes with the parish priest. She received this impression chiefly from the following incident. She had put to the form the question (I remember the exact words): 'How do we think of Our Lord?' Amid the expected answers of 'teacher', 'miracle-worker', 'saviour', I thought it was interesting to note that he was invariably thought of as handsome. Mother B commented that she thought some additional RI lessons might benefit me.

The values instilled by the convent were associated with the three cups awarded each year to the houses that had done best in study, service and games. Games were regarded as the least important of these areas, at least by our form, which was very bad at them and thought they were a consolation for the dimmer streams. Nowhere was games enthusiasm allowed to get out of hand. The headmistress once had to remind the school in assembly that during house matches clapping was permitted, but cheering and stamping the feet were not suitable for convent girls. Study, too, had a certain sickly air. Originality and imagination were not highly regarded, and brilliance was never sought after. On the whole application to study was more praised than actual achievement, and received more prizes at speech day. 'Application to study' was not quite the same as working hard: it also implied working in the right spirit of co-operation.

Service, however, was the real heart of virtue. Not for nothing did we wear 'Serviam' embroidered on our blazer pockets. Service marks were awarded to those who had voluntarily given extra help in clearing away after dinner, or in putting out or putting away chairs in the hall. 'Stella is very holy: she always does the chairs' was a remark I remember. In the nuns' vocabulary, the opposite of 'service' was 'selfishness'. One of the best ways of conquering this vice, we were told, was to use the word 'I' less often in conversation. Disorderly classes were brought to order with the command 'Stop being so selfish'. Girls who talked in corridors or hid in the cloakrooms during break to have secret tête-à-têtes were also called selfish. Sometimes selfishness came very close to individuality.

After my first year at the convent, which I did not enjoy, for reasons I found impossible to articulate, I fell violently in love with a senior girl. From now on I went eagerly to school, and also made daily visits to chapel in the lunch break, as this afforded me a regular opportunity of passing the dining hall while my beloved was having her lunch.

Although half our class had crushes, mine was the most famous, and probably the most intense. I even had the distinction of being reprimanded by the headmistress for silly behaviour. Every page of my rough book was inscribed with my beloved's name, lovingly embellished in one style or another. Once a term, not more, I spoke to her, as I wished her a happy Christmas, or Easter, or summer holiday. While the rest of the class were writing suitable free verse about the beauty of gardens and the sunshine, I was producing frightful, naive love poetry like this:

> Thou, sweet A., art my love,
> Thou gentle one, thou perfect dove;
> With hair so black and back so straight
> And lively voice that none can hate,
> Thy fate is to be loved by me,
> How am I worthy to love thee?
> Although you'll one day be a wife
> You are at the moment my whole life.

Twelve, then, was for me an age of relative conformity in one area (liking school) brought about by a cause (love) that was viewed with suspicion and disapproval. The following year my excessive passion had worn off, and I consequently became intolerable at school, it having become intolerable for me. My interests were Shakespeare and Keats, and I could find no one among either girls or staff to share my enthusiasm. I spent all my pocket money on going to the theatre, almost invariably alone, and I did not know how to drag through the years till I would be legally permitted to leave school. I showed my disdain for the hateful place by refusing to do my homework, and by being at least twenty minutes late almost every morning. If you were so late as to miss part of the first lesson as well as assembly, you had to make your excuses to the headmistress, and it must have been exceedingly tedious for her as I trudged in day after day. As for me, the unpleasant incident beginning each day made school even worse than it would otherwise have been. To make a resolution to arrive on time, however, would have implied acceptance and compromise, so I went on making life awful for myself and for the nuns, who found they could do nothing with me. At this time religion meant very little, being almost exclusively associated with an institution that I considered conformist and mediocre.

The following year I discovered the appeal of the intellectual, and consequently began to find some interest in my school work. There was no intellectual area that riveted my attention more now than religion. I swiftly became an agnostic, by the following merciless logic: not everyone believes in God, let alone in the Christian God; how can I possibly know that I am right and they are wrong, when it is not a matter of drawing conclusions from unambiguous evidence?; therefore I must say I do not know whether or not God exists. By now I had found some fellow spirits among my schoolmates, but very little interest or understanding from the teachers of religion. Metaphysical discussion became an occupation of endless fascination and of decisive importance. The nuns, however, seemed to regard this new unbelief, and the attempt to spread it, as merely another instance of my irreformable naughtiness.

There were occasions when I was singled out from the whole school for especial reproach. One of these instances was when I had giggled uncontrollably through an earnest and fierily delivered admonition made to the whole assembly by the head girl. We were told off for sloppy behaviour, sloppy dress, 'and', she finished thunderingly, 'some of you even chew gum'. On the other occasion I was summoned to the second mistress's office. As one of my friends remarked, she always spoke as though she had a hot potato in her mouth. 'You have just nearly burned down the general library', she said. 'We might have had a fleet of fire engines in the road outside. Fortunately a girl discovered the room full of smoke while the fire was still confined to the wastepaper basket.' What I had done was to use a paper spill to light the gas fire in the adjoining room, and thrown it away in the bin. I was sent to chapel to say a decade of the rosary in thanksgiving for the saving of the general library. I had in fact mixed feelings about this near-miss, because I had always considered the general library a dump of old-fashioned and generally worthless books, as the nuns well knew since we had to write reviews of books we had borrowed. I was also aware that to have burned down one of your school buildings would be rather distinguished in later life. However, on balance I felt a little relieved that the incident had been exciting but not actually serious.

It was perhaps an indication of some fellow feeling that we subsequently chose for our eldest child's godmother a girl who had been expelled from her convent school for setting fire to the Reverend Mother. What she really wanted to do, she explained, was to set the hose on her, and she felt it would mitigate this crime if she was putting out a fire in the process. So she put a match to the back of the Reverend Mother's veil, and when it had just taken light she turned the hose on her, full blast, top to toe, driving off her veil and making her run sadly off, her feet squelching in her watery shoes.

My son's godmother and I were not merely having a bit of fun playing up our schoolmistresses — there was a deeper and more disturbing element than that. It was no coincidence that these nuns called themselves Mothers. Although they were not very close to any of their pupils in terms of affection, they tried to be very authoritative in terms of up-bringing. It was their prerogative to educate us in our faith, adjudicate over the virtues, and prepare us for woman-hood. And yet we felt they neither understood nor were interested in our questions, and failed to provide for our spiritual needs. Motherhood is not an easy model for a teacher of adolescents: it is just the age when a girl cuts loose from her mother and laughs at her, and so did we to these surrogate mothers. So long as they were prepared to put a bright smiling face on the world, we were prepared to torment them. Later, under the influence of Vatican II, they changed their names to Sister, and took up their hems three inches. If I met them now I think we could be good friends, precisely because it would not be an attempt at a mother–daughter relationship. In fact I have met three of them in recent years, just by chance. Although it is more than ten years later, they all amazed me by looking ten years younger than when I last saw them. Something very strange has been happening to nuns.

When I was nearing the end of my fourth year at the convent there occurred the turning point in my religious history. Three Jesuits came to the school for a week to give a retreat. Our year was granted one day out of the week. Since I was an agnostic but very interested in religious questions I felt I should ask permission to attend. This was grudgingly granted with warnings about not wanting anyone to spoil it for the others. The three Jesuits were young, handsome, energetic, uttered exclamations like 'Mon Dieu', spoke of the spirituality of risk, and played the guitar. The whole school was utterly bowled over. I was converted on the first morning. Aware as I was even at the time of the possible 'explanations' for such a conversion, I believed, and still do, that it was genuine. The persuasive circumstances enabled, but did not account for, a gift of faith that I have never subsequently doubted. With great relief I made a confession, was able to receive communion again, and announced to all that I had been converted. The nuns laughed in disbelief.

My days burned with the desire to give my life wholly to God. How to do this seemed a bit problematic, since I had understood that giving your life wholly to God meant — in the case of a woman — becoming a nun. If I had been a man there would evidently have been less of a problem, but I really did not believe that my calling was to a convent. 'I think it is just possible that you might have a vocation', said one of the Jesuits, meaning it nicely. In those days the term 'vocation' needed no explanatory qualification. I did not try to tell him that the nuns had filled me with not a single religious sentiment in my life.

What this book is about is how I am trying to resolve that problem, of how to be a fully committed Christian and a lay woman in my specific calling of motherhood. It sounds so silly now to think that giving your life to God means being a religious in the technical sense, and yet fifteen years ago the terms were used almost synonymously. Even today we have hardly begun to do more than affirm the reality, in theory, of the lay vocation. We have barely begun to explore the spirituality of motherhood, and the influence it makes on theology. We are only just starting to work out how to give the laity their rightful opportunities for religious development, and how to gather from them their privileged insights into God. This book tries to be an early step on the way.

Part One

2

Wanting children

Between leaving behind the nunny mothers (at the age of sixteen) and becoming a mother myself (at the age of twenty-five) naturally quite a lot happened, most of it of dubious relevance to this book, which is not intended to be an autobiography but simply to draw on personal experience when necessary.

But being a mother is for me inextricably intertwined with my relationship with Peter, my husband. For me, the question of having a family only came up within the context of my marriage, and my children's daily presence with us now continually refers back to that relationship. That is to put it mildly. They are Peter's children: they look like him, they behave like him, they live with him and they love him, and if in this book I speak almost always of the mother and hardly ever of the father, that is simply because it is motherhood I have chosen to talk about.

Motherhood is not an isolated relationship; for some people, unmarried mothers or abandoned wives, it may seem so, but it has always sprung out of a relationship with a man. A woman comes to being a mother out of a whole background of living and loving that places her maternity in context. For me that context was, is and always will be Peter.

When we married we always knew we would want to have children, but for the first few years we wanted to be alone. Even the most discreet baby would have deprived us of the joy of relaxed aloneness together. It was a joy that seemed endless at the time, although we knew that slowly, imperceptibly we would move towards that point at which we could say with spontaneous sincerity 'Now we are ready to have a child'. That was exactly how it happened.

After a couple of years we were in the car one day, going round a particular roundabout close to our home, and for some reason that I do not recall the question of children came up. Suddenly we were both aware that we now felt ready for them; our love had had space and freedom in which to uncoil, to stretch, to become aware of itself, and at last was ready to move into a new phase.

What was it that we wanted in wanting children? We wanted to share our love, to bring other human beings into the light and warmth of an existence that was founded on love, to give something of what we had received, of the joy that we felt almost guilty to relish alone. We wanted also the sweetness and charm of childhood, little voices, little pitter-pattering feet, miniature garments hanging out to dry on the line or folded away in little chests of drawers; a children's room, with Winnie the Pooh calendars and nursery curtains and a little shelf of picture books; teddy bears and bath toys, tricycles and baby chairs, making up part of the furniture and feel of the house. Perhaps most of all we wanted to create, to make something much greater than a book or a home or any other creative product; we wanted to make a person, a real, living human person, to call it into existence from nothingness, and leave it behind us as our joint legacy to the world. It would be a person who looked like us, like both of us at the same time, in an un-imaginable new combination — a miraculous embodi-ment, literal embodiment, of a love that looked for express-ion. It would live after we had died, it would, we hoped, have children itself, and so our love, which we felt was so great, would leave a lasting mark on humanity, not just by a spiritual influence, but in a living, personal, tangible way. We would be co-operators with God in creation, privileged to contribute to the new world with flesh of our flesh, love of our love, life of our life.

Little wonder that God is so often thought of under the image of parent. The very fact of being our creator makes us turn immediately to the associated idea of parent. Can it be that God has created each one of us in the longing to share her joy with us, to call us forth into the warmth of the love that she knows and wants to spread to others? Can it be that God's love is so powerful, so restless and explosive that all the billions of people who have ever lived have not exhausted her drive to express it again and again? Can it be that God finds us as endearing to look at, in all our adult gaucheness, as we find little children, with their perfect skins and fine hair and unblemished bodies? Does it fill God with enchantment to gaze at us her children? Does she see our houses and offices and roads not as blurs on the beauty of her creation, but as the evocative traces of the children she adores, as charming as the children's paintings we pin on our walls? Is she proud of our clumsy, ugly efforts? When we say God made us in her own image (Gen 1:27) can we believe she is as pleased at the sight of herself in us as we are when we see our features mirrored in our children? Does she look forward to our children, as we look forward to our children's children? Can we believe all this?

Christian doctrine authorizes us to do so: God's love surpasses our wildest imaginings, being infinite. Sometimes we are more affected by reducing it to the finite, to something that we can grasp, or almost grasp, something that does not stand apart in the abstraction of theory but joins with the strands of parental love that, though merely human, are known powerfully enough within us.

After we had finally decided we wanted a child we waited a few months longer for me to take my exams while I still felt well, and then we set about trying to get me pregnant. Unfortunately we discovered it was not as automatic as we had imagined. Babies might be able to be stopped by order, but could not be started by order. The frustration was immense. For my part, now my studies were over, I did not know whether I should look for a job. It was the last thing I wanted; what I wanted was a baby. How long should I hang on unemployed, with nothing to occupy my thoughts other than the expected date of my next ovulation? But how unfair it would be to any employer to take a job in the hope that within a week or two I might be able to hand in my notice. When people said 'How are you?' I would feel evasive as I said 'Very well, thank you' while my internal voice answered 'Well I am eight days past what I think was my date of ovulation, that means I might actually be pregnant though I will not even have any grounds for hoping for at least another six or seven days;

even supposing I was late I would have to wait a further week or ten days before I could have a test; so it is just possible that in about thirteen days time I might find I was pregnant, on the other hand if I'm not I will have to wait about twenty days or more till I have even another chance; meanwhile I keep on looking for signs of sickness but I cannot say I have noticed anything to speak of, on the other hand it would be much too early for that anyway so that does not show anything . . . '. But all this was quite internal, quite secret, and all my external self would show was a slight smile that tried not to look too weary.

The longing for a baby grew as the months passed and nothing happened. Alone together we felt increasingly solitary, in company we felt constrained to keep silence on our sole preoccupation, that was rapidly becoming a worry. A whole new field of human suffering was opened to our eyes — the pain of infertility. How unjust it seemed that good and loving couples who actually longed for babies should find themselves infertile. Barrenness, sterility, fruitlessness, infertility — all these words acquired an emotional meaning for me that I had never dreamed of, brought up in a twentieth-century world that thinks so much of the problems of reducing conceptions and so little of the problems of bringing them about. Just as when I was a teenager the unmarried mother state seemed to me to sum up human disaster and sadness, so now the childless wife state took on that role. Compared to being forever without children, how small seemed the disaster of having one too soon. How small too the disadvantages of having too many. Better thirteen children than none at all. The world changed under my eyes. When I went to the supermarket my eyes could pick out straight away which tummies were beginning to swell with a child, and amid so many housewives there were always one or two on each visit. What a blessed state pregnancy seemed.

My worries were unfounded. Early medical enquiries were reassuring, and one doctor had the sense to suggest that our preoccupation with scientific precision might be disturbing the delicate balance of body chemistry. I threw away my thermometer, and conceived the next month. When the time came to conceive our subsequent children, we had no problem. But the experience taught me about an area of human suffering that I had practically ignored. The statistics of infertility, I discovered, are staggeringly high, even in countries with sophisticated medicine. It is still a major problem.

I also learnt a certain humility about our ability to create life. Choosing to have a baby is not simply within our power. We can open up that possibility, we can go a long way towards enabling it to happen, but we cannot dictate it. In the end it is God who gives life, and every now and again she reminds us of it. There is a truth in the version of the gooseberry bush myth I believed as a child. 'How do you get a baby?' 'You pray for it.' There is a very profound truth about our dependence on God, in this field especially, in which we can be co-operators in God's creating, but not ourselves creators.

3

Expecting a baby

When I found I was pregnant I was radiant with happiness. I had had the test done in a basement clinic in central London, and I wandered out in a daze and into a big department store, where I straight away bought a dozen nappies and a woolly bonnet. I queued at the shop snack bar for lunch; it was a long queue, and that gave me all the more time to relish my condition. Here am I, I thought, in line with so many other women, and yet I am different, I am pregnant. No one can see it, only I know it, but I have something so secret and precious inside me. I basked in a glow of blessedness. I had no fears and no doubts.

Nine months is a long time for enjoying the knowledge that you are pregnant, but for me it was not a day too long. I had a tremendous sense of physical fulfilment, and I saw my body move into a new stage of development for which it had waited since puberty. Within a few weeks I had read all the latest books on pregnancy from cover to cover several times over, and had enrolled myself — or rather ourselves, for husbands were expected at all sessions — for a course of natural childbirth classes with England's leading teacher, Sheila Kitzinger. Meanwhile my body slowly evolved.

I soon became aware of the disagreeable symptoms of the first trimester. I never felt sick, but instead a debilitating tiredness took me over, like the apathetic physical low that follows in the wake of flu. I did not want to go out, and if out I wanted to come home. I could not drink coffee: I found the taste so unpleasant that I could not finish a cup even out of politeness. Alcohol also became disagreeable. But through this early stage of pregnancy — surely the worst for most women — my spirits were buoyed up by the awareness of the little being inside me, and I followed its development carefully week by week with the aid of books, as features formed, fingers separated, eyelids opened.

By the fourth month I could clearly see that my tummy was lumpier than usual and I had the delight of moving into pregnancy dresses, which I found flowing and romantic. At the same time I began to feel absolutely marvellous — not just back to form, but glowing with health and energy. From now on I was on the home run, and even the backache and varicose veins that accompanied my last months were amply compensated for by the satisfying size of my tummy. I loved going out, being seen to be pregnant, displaying the fruits of my husband's love and sex with me in a way that could not possibly be thought immodest. I felt like a caterpillar that has at last achieved its true destiny of emerging from its chrysalis to stretch its beautiful, new, butterfly wings; or like the ugly duckling who finally sheds its dark feathers to discover itself the most graceful and shining of all birds.

Such images have also been used to describe our future, risen bodies. Paul writes 'the dead will be raised imperishable, and we shall be changed. For this perishable nature must put on the imperishable, and this mortal nature must put on immortality' (1 Cor 15:52–53). Often in the past I have felt uncomfortable with this idea of a new body that is ours, yet different: in so far as it is different it has seemed not truly a body, and not truly mine, and yet it could not be the same as now if it belonged to eternity.

Perhaps it can be understood a little through the parallel with pregnancy: though we cannot imagine it in advance, perhaps when it happens it will have the same feel of rightness and fulfilment, as though the whole development of our earthly bodies has been a sort of puberty preparing us for the moment when in a truly physical way we shall move into a new phase. We shall find our bodies able to do things we never thought they could, a little bit like the way in pregnancy the whole metabolism switches into a new gear, and works bigger and better than ever, nourishing and feeding not one but two bodies, or like the way we find our tummies can stretch to an extent we would never have believed possible had we not seen it in others, or like the way our bodies can open up to give birth to the fully grown baby — how could we have imagined that there would be room for a whole baby to come out in one piece if we had not the experience of others to go on? Maybe our new risen bodies will have that feel of unexpectedly fulfilled physicality, so that when we materialize and dematerialize (as the risen Christ did) we will feel not less ourselves, but more than ever ourselves.

As I neared the end of my pregnancy I began to feel certain anxieties that had been quite absent from the earlier euphoria. I became less aware of my present state merely as a thing in itself, more aware of the unknown before me. I have a memory, about the fourth month, of a friend giving me a lot of toddler clothes, and of me saying 'It is so hard to believe that I am ever going to have a tiny baby, but to believe it will ever be big enough to wear these is practically impossible'. As I neared my delivery I still found it hard to believe there was a baby inside me about to come out. I could feel it kicking of course, and bits of legs or bottom would push my tummy out from time to time, altering the contour. But, laws of induction aside, I would have found it easier to believe I had some lesser form of life within me, like a rabbit for instance, rather than an actual human baby. I lacked confidence in my capabilities to produce anything so marvellous as a human being.

If I did bridge that gap of credibility I imagined the baby as ugly. In one of my late pregnancy dreams I had left the baby on a train. I had to walk miles to find it, and as I walked I could not remember what it looked like. At last I came to a shop of babies, and there it was — immediately recognizable as the one with abnormally large feet. I reclaimed it happily, glad there was nothing worse wrong with it.

At the back of every woman's mind is the fear of a deformed or handicapped child. It was at the back of my mind too, but not excessively so. I was more afraid in a general way that I would reject my child — that I simply would not like what turned up. At least adoptive parents can give a baby a look over before deciding if they can love it. I would have no choice. No choice and no escape.

Such anxieties, natural enough surely, perhaps universal

in some degree, did not destroy my mood of confident expectation, but rather lived alongside it. I still enjoyed my intimate communion with the wriggling being in my tummy. In fact it was easier to love it just as a wriggling unborn than as a future imaginary baby. I liked the closeness of having it inside me, I liked the physicality of our knowledge of each other, touching without seeing. I liked to think of the warmth and security I was giving it in my womb, where all its needs were met immediately and painlessly along the umbilical cord. It was good to be able to give in this way, simply by being. Without even thinking about it I was giving indispensable support and safeness, and knowing that made me glad, and being glad made me love the being I was able to help. I tried sometimes to send willed waves of love and acceptance towards it inside me. Perhaps that did not help, but it was rather like a prayer — a commitment of my will to an aspiration genuinely felt but still half-hearted and weakened by doubt. I was saying to my baby 'I want to do all I can to help you, and if you are affected now by my feelings towards you I would like those feelings to be as loving as can possibly be'.

If we are God's children it might be helpful to imagine ourselves sometimes as in her womb. There could not be a closer image of warmth, security and protection. There we have all our needs provided for in perfect measure, as the baby receives oxygen and nourishment without deficiency or excess through the umbilical cord. In God's womb we can stretch and turn in every direction, just as the baby, suspended in water, is as happy upside down as the right way up, and in the early months can exercise its limbs freely. Wherever God our mother takes us we will be safe and provided for; whether in cold or heat, storm or drought, we will be protected. Wherever we journey to we will still be at home, for the presence of our mother's body is closer to us than our geographical location. God is closer to us than the ground we stand on. Even though we have never seen our mother, perhaps are quite unaware of her, or even deny her existence, she is in perfect and constant intimacy with us, and when we are born into the light of her presence we will recognize that she has been with us all along.

4

Lessons for childbirth

A few months before the Estimated Date of Delivery Peter and I began to attend Sheila Kitzinger's evening classes in preparation for childbirth. Sheila Kitzinger has been called 'the high priestess of transcendental maternity' and she lives up to the title with panache. Her sitting room is furnished with large modern paintings, a huge stone fireplace, and a commodious selection of cushy sofas and sagbags, on which, once a week, sprawl a group of big-bellied women fantasizing the moments of their approaching labour. At the side of each crouches a husband, with one hand giving her a good, sharp pinch in the upper thigh to simulate a contraction, with the other stroking her softly while he tries to murmur words of encouragement. Over the top of these quiet words are heard sounds of breathing, recognizable by the initiates as falling into several different categories: 'the greeting breath', slow full-chest breathing, quicker shallow-chest breathing, mouth-centred breathing, 'sheep's breathing', the quick blow, 'breathing it all away' and so on.

Sheila has drawn her inspiration from a variety of sources. 'I call it sheep's breathing', she said, 'because I learnt it from a sheep' — a sheep in labour whom she came across one night as she was walking over an Oxfordshire field. Another source is Stanislavsky, famous for his school of acting known as Method, in which vividly detailed fantasy plays an important part in preparing for a role. There seems to be a bit of Eastern influence too somewhere, something that reminds one of Indian yogis lying in calm serenity on beds of nails. Her stress on physical togetherness of mother and child comes partly from the anthropology of child-rearing in developing countries. Most notably, of course, she is indebted to her own predecessors in natural childbirth training, especially Doctors Dick-Read and Lamaze. Finally, there is a good sprinkling of consumer awareness, most explicitly expressed in her *Good Birth Guide* (Fontana, London and Glasgow, 1979; rev. ed. Penguin Books, Harmondsworth, 1983), which will tell you all you want to know about any maternity hospital in Britain.

It would be difficult to imagine a more physically sumptuous approach than Sheila's. I once saw a few shots on television of another kind of natural childbirth class. A sort of gym mistress in a white coat was calling out orders of 'in . . . out' before a neat row of identical mattresses on the floor. The tummies were all there one behind the other in line. Sheila's classes could not be more different. She appears in a long flowing dress with her hair pinned up and welcomes each couple individually. The husbands are urged to make their wives comfortable with lots of cushions, maybe even going upstairs to the big four-poster bed for another armful of pillows. If you are the wife you begin to feel rather special straight away. Sheila speaks well, enthusiastically and soothingly at the same time, encouraging you to call up your favourite images to help you relax . . . . I soon felt I was lying happily on a sun-drenched beach on a tropical island, drinking expensive champagne, eating mangoes and attended by a sole, adoring man. No wonder you get the idea that there is going to be something rather nice about being in labour. Meanwhile Sheila is telling you how 'deliciously luxurious' she felt, relaxing between the contractions of her third or fourth labour. Or she is having everyone try to wag their tail. Now I did not know I had a tail until I went to Sheila's classes, and even when I knew I was not at all sure that I had managed to wag it, but Sheila came round saying 'Put your finger here, feel me do it', and at once we began to feel that body control was going to be fun. Or another time Sheila told us how she painted the staircase blue in a wild burst of energy known as 'nesting' that immediately preceded one labour; and she was so keen on her painting that she put on the second coat without waiting for it to dry, so that when her children came up to see the new baby they all had blue toes. And then she would recommend to us 'making love very passionately' as a good way of provoking an overdue labour, and 'a long, loving kiss on the mouth' to help the perineum relax prior to crowning.

But it is not all Sheila talking, even if her remarks are the most memorable element. She brings along to the class the new graduates, as it were, from the last series, mothers and fathers of a mere week or two's standing, so that they can recount with freshness and uncensored honesty how it worked out in practice. From them we learned that it is not always as straightforward and controllable as you would like it to be. We heard first-hand experiences, fresh in the memory, of long labours and snappy doctors, of induced births and jabs of pethidine, of bothersome stitches and babies who would not suck. But from them all, easy or difficult, with drugs or without, came a strong wave of positive feeling, so that we felt encouraged to face the unexpected and the problematic with confidence, as well of course as the simply painful. And most encouraging of all was that little baby, whom Sheila always had passed round. It was so small, so funny and sweet and so light to hold, and we passed it very quickly, fearing that if we held it more than a minute it would start to cry or we might drop it.

By the time we had finished the classes we were all looking forward to our labour. One girl was lucky enough to start real contractions in earnest actually during the last class. Another girl whose dates had been sooner came and sat at her feet and said 'I am so jealous'. One of the others was warned to be prepared for a particularly long labour because the baby was the wrong way round. Sheila asked her how she felt about it and she said 'It is a challenge'. Two of the husbands got cameras ready to record the beautiful moments to come in unexpurgated detail. And we all packed our suitcases several weeks earlier than necessary. When my time eventually came my midwife was fascinated and amused by the variety of gear I had included. 'What's this for?' she asked as she held up one strange object after another. 'Ah, that's an idea of Sheila Kitzinger's. It's a garden spray, so that Peter can cool down my face with a fine spray of cold water. That's another idea of Sheila's — it's an ice pack such as is used for picnics, but if it is stood in hot water for a while it can be used like a hot water bottle. That's the notebook and pencil, so that Peter can keep a written record of the length of each contraction and the spaces between them. That's some talcum powder — it helps in massage. That's a pair of bed-socks, for the "shivering legs" stage. That's my favourite perfume — it's meant to keep up morale if I get hot and tired.' I began to feel rather over-prepared, but fortunately the name 'Kitzinger' draws great respect from midwives.

Did it help? I never used any of the gadgets, but the techniques of breathing and relaxation, the encouragement and the sheer information about what was likely to happen were quite indispensable. They did not stop the pain, but they enabled me to cope with it so that I was completely undrugged and wide awake for the only bit I actually enjoyed — the welcoming of the baby into my arms. I would not have missed that for the world, but more of that in the next chapter.

More generally, I learned through the principle of relaxation an approach not just to the pains of childbirth, not just to physical pain of any kind, but to mental and spiritual pain as well. When we are hurt, whether physically or emotionally, our first response is to clam up. We must learn to give, to open, to trust. We need conscious practice in relaxing in the face of the unpleasant and unknown. A Christian believes all of life's hurts are part of a birth process, as we are opened up to the new life to which God calls us. Our call is not to resist, but to understand the pain positively, as a giving-birth and even as a beautiful process, in which we are not the oppressed but the privileged. God touches our mouth with burning coal in order to purify us and prepare us for a new mission, and so we must give ourselves into God's hands without holding back from the experience or tensing up against what is initially unwelcome:

> Then flew one of the seraphim to me, having in
> his hand a burning coal which he had taken with
> tongs from the altar. And he touched my mouth,
> and said: 'Behold, this has touched your lips;
> your guilt is taken away, and your sin forgiven.'

And I heard the voice of the Lord saying, 'Whom shall I send, and who will go for us?' Then I said, 'Here am I! Send me' (Is 6:6–8).

Prayer is a practice in this, an exercise for the unknown moment. Fantasies can be used with great profit in prayer, just as they are used in the preparation for childbirth. The Indian Jesuit Anthony de Mello, whose book of prayer exercises *Sadhana — A Way to God* (Gujarat Sahitya Prakash, Anand, India, 1978) became a world best-seller almost as soon as it was published, makes great use of fantasy. He has found fantasies of the past, for example, valuable for healing hurtful memories, fantasies of the future helpful for preparing us to meet our fears of illness and death. Fantasies of conversing with Jesus, present in the room with us, can help us discover our true feelings. Fantasies of being present with him at events in the gospels can bring us into a deeper response to these mysteries.

Physical relaxation and trust is at least a bodily complement to the spiritual giving of ourselves to God; at best it can actually form part of a state of prayer. St Dominic was particularly fond of using his body as a way of speaking to God or deepening his spiritual responses. He would throw himself flat on the ground when he wanted to express repentance; he would kneel and rise, kneel and rise for hours on end as a prayer for inner cleaning; stretching out his arms in the form of a cross or up above his head he would make prayers of deep entreaty. What then could be more suitable than to use relaxation exercises as a gesture of self-giving and trust in God? Usually we kneel or sit to pray, but why not just lie down and melt into the loving arms of God, giving her our will even as we give her our body? If we have already learned relaxation as part of natural childbirth it will be a good way of integrating the aims and experiences of our life: in offering ourselves we will be bringing along memories and associations that are already important to us and that we need to lay before God.

In fact in my second and third labours I did consciously combine childbirth techniques with prayer. Sheila had spoken of the value of 'focused concentration' as a way of distracting ourselves from the force of the contractions.

She had suggested focusing on a picture on the wall, on an imaginary sequence of colours, or on a mental recitation of the alphabet. I chose to say the Lord's Prayer. It felt very right that even as I concentrated on means to help me through the contractions I should at the same time be asking God's help ('Deliver us from evil') and giving myself into her hands ('Thy will be done'). I had found a way in which I could welcome God's coming as I welcomed my child's coming.

5

The first birth

I chose to have my first child in the General Practitioner unit of our local maternity hospital, which meant I had a chance to get to know the midwives and doctors who would look after me beforehand and to check that we saw eye-to-eye on natural childbirth. It also meant that the midwives would come to my house for the early stages of labour, so that I could stay for much longer in the comfort and privacy of my own home.

The start of labour is not always easy to pinpoint. I had had the odd 'practice contraction' for a week beforehand. It would wake me in the night and I would get all alert, waiting to put my breathing into operation. But there would not be another one and I would lie awake for a couple of hours before giving up hope and going to sleep again. Then one morning I started a regular sequence of little flutters, but they were far too light even to need breathing through and certainly were not doing anything other than letting me know my time was close.

After lunch, I really got going. Peter looked excited and proud that the moment had come for him to play a part. He went off to ring the midwife and came back with confident reassurances that she was coming over straight away. He got out the notebook and started to time the contractions as he had been taught. The midwife arrived sooner than I could have believed possible. She brought with her a student from Malaysia. They were both flushed and delighted, and got down to work with enthusiasm. They had to time the contractions, do an internal examination to assess progress, shave me and give me a suppository to clear out my bowels. Then we settled down to wait. The contractions seemed fairly strong but did not achieve very much: the baby was slightly turned sideways and that was holding up the dilatation of the cervix. I began to feel it might be a long and tough haul.

Then after a urine test they said I was dehydrated and would have to go to hospital to have a glucose drip put in my arm. For the first time I felt afraid as Peter wrapped a long cloak over my nightdress and led me out to the car. I had reached the point that I had been told about so often — the moment when you realize there is no way back, no possibility of having a rest and trying again another day. The only way through this labour is forward, through stronger contractions and more exhaustion until the baby is born. The car was a Mini and I felt cramped on the back seat next to the student midwife. It was dark now, and we had to take a diversion to avoid the St Giles fair that occupies the main thoroughfare of Oxford for two days in early September. We could hear the fairground music as we skirted north.

When we reached the hospital I had another internal examination in a preparation room. It took a long time, and the midwife looked thoughtful. Through the open window came sounds of shouting and cheering from an evening match at Oxford United football ground. It was a suitable sound to form the background to a labour — their blood was up, their cries were fixed on their goal. Then the midwife said they would break my waters. I was afraid: I had learned from the classes that the breaking of the waters signals the approach of even stronger contractions, and I honestly did not think I could take anything more. I took the chance, while the midwives were out of the room for a moment, to say to Peter 'I think I am going to have to have something'. He said nothing, but in his eyes he hoped it would not be necessary.

There are two ways in which medicine can relieve the pain of labour. One is an epidural, in which anaesthetic is fed into the spinal cavity, and all sensation goes from that point downwards: you watch the birth of your baby like a detached observer and feel no pain at all. It is an effective measure, but many women feel it is too extreme: they want to have a sense of giving birth, experienced in their own sensations. The alternative is an injection of a drug known as pethidine. It can be given in various doses, and has certainly given many women just that little bit of help to get through the hardest stages. But it has drawbacks: it induces a sense of sleepiness, that has even formed a hindrance to some women coached in natural childbirth techniques, because they are too tired to get together the breathing and conscious relaxation that is sometimes more help than the pethidine itself. It also reaches the baby — unlike the epidural — so that the baby is slightly drugged when it emerges: it may not breathe so soon on exposure to the air, but no hospital would give a dose that really formed a danger to the child. It is not an easy choice between an epidural or pethidine or hanging on on your own. I preferred to do without, but I was afraid that with my progress so slow and the baby not yet turned I would not be able to last the long hours ahead. But for the moment I said nothing to the midwives.

The student midwife broke my waters. It was evidently the first time she had done this, and it took her a very long time. Shortly after this I completely lost control of the pain, and I moaned and flailed in desperation. I got Peter to put his hand on my tummy during the contractions, and that communicated some kind of warmth and calm and comfort, but I cannot pretend I was in any way able to cope with pain on this level. The midwife went off to ring the doctor — quite unalarmed. As far as medical judgements went, everything was quite in order.

I was wheeled on my bed into the delivery room, and the doctor arrived in white rubber boots as well as the pre-scribed overalls and funny hat that even Peter had to put on. The doctor made some bright remark from the door. I was having a contraction at the time and did not hear what he said though I knew he was talking. Then he wandered over and said 'Is she uncomfortable?' Even in my pain I was faintly amused by this understatement. I said 'I am going to be like this for hours, aren't I?' 'Look', he said, 'we just don't know when the baby will turn. It could turn any time. In half an hour it could turn. Who knows?' I went into another contraction and writhed and gasped. 'Where does it hurt?' he said. 'Down here', I said, pointing to my bum. 'It can't be hurting down there already', he said, 'When did you last examine her?' 'Just before I rang you', said the midwife, and bent down to have a peep. She stood up in delight. 'Yes', she said, 'you are in the second stage. The baby is coming out.' 'No wonder she was uncomfortable', said the doctor.

The second stage of labour starts when the neck of the womb is fully dilated. It is far shorter and more satisfying than the long, tiring first stage, because with every contraction the baby actually inches its way forward towards the world, and the woman can consciously join her efforts to the involuntary contractions to push the baby out. What had happened to me was that those recent, violent pains had not only turned the baby but completed the rest of the long dilatation process in the space of a few minutes. I was glad now that I had hung on without pethidine. A dose of pethidine would not even have started to work until the baby was practically born, and I would have gone drowsy at just the moment I wanted to wake up.

From now on we were all eager and the midwives could see with their own eyes the progress of each contraction. Peter took one arm, the doctor the other, and the two midwives hung about at the receiving end. One held a mirror so I could watch. (I had learnt from my classes that you could ask for this.) 'This dark thing', they said, 'is the head of the baby.' You could have fooled me. I could not even see a dark thing, and I could not believe that such an imaginary shadow was a real baby's head. After a couple more contractions I could see they were right. Then the head 'crowned' — in my case popping out like a cork. The next contraction had the baby propelled out into the safe hands of the Malaysian student. 'It's a boy!' they cried, and he howled straight away. They put him on my tummy, all wet and smeary and red, and his little face wrinkled up in protesting cries. 'Dominic Paul', I said, caressing him, 'it's all right, it's all right', the tears coursing down my face, even as they do now as I remember it. The unbelievable had happened, and I was filled with joy.

Of course everyone had told me I was going to have a baby. The statistics had assured me of the overwhelming probability that it would be alive and well. The experience of others had proved that mothers do love their babies when they arrive. But I could not believe it in my heart. I could not believe that I could produce something as wonderful as a human being. I could not believe that such a great gift would be given me, or that, if given, I would welcome it. I had doubted my ability to love this new creature, although I had longed for it so much. And now I could not hesitate any more, my last resistances of distrust and self-doubt were wiped away as I looked with my own eyes on this new creation that was mine and that I loved at once. 'And God saw everything that he had made, and behold, it was very good' (Gen 1:31). To see what you have made coming forth from within you, and in that moment of first vision, to love it totally and for always . . . . Can anyone who has not given birth, in fact or in imagination, understand what it means for God to have created us? And will the sight of God in heaven be like this, when after unbearable pain and waiting the hidden is made known? Will we weep with relief from fears that we barely knew we had, fears that we would not like God when we saw her, that she would not be to our taste, distant, puritanical and boring, or frightening and unsympathetic? Will we have the sense I had when I saw Dominic, that this being was at once totally new and unforeseeable, and yet totally the answer to the desire I had felt? It is perhaps as close as we can come to imagining the impact of the beatific vision.

Not all mothers fall in love with their babies at first sight. For some the love comes more slowly, over the next few days or weeks. But even that is sudden enough to upturn your life in the shock of a new love. You will never be the same again, and you are full of wonder as you find yourself anew as a woman with a new gift of love.

What happened to those background fears of a handicapped baby? When you are introduced to someone you do not think to give them a quick look over for any deformities, you take it for granted that they are normal. It was the same seeing Dominic — I took it for granted that he was normal. And indeed he was. If only I could have had that trust all through the pregnancy, that when I saw him I would cry out at his loveliness, not look him over for any fault, then I could have looked forward to his birth without anxiety. But even after the first experience I still had doubts the second and third time round.

Everyone knows the words of Jesus in John's gospel: 'When a woman is in travail she has sorrow, because her hour has come; but when she is delivered of the child, she no longer remembers the anguish, for joy that a child is born into the world' (Jn 16:21). When Peter made his first proud visit to the hospital the next day he picked up a New Testament and read that verse to me again, because it was so right. It is not a question of forgetting altogether the experiences that had been painful, but of seeing them in a new light. The pain is so recent, and yet one single event has achieved as much as years of internal assimilation in rendering it harmless. If we remember our labour it is in a new way, reliving it with a new life, so that we do not need to shut anything from our consciousness, because we see it all from the other side of the end. The pain becomes like the wounds in the body of the risen Christ (Jn 20:27; Lk 24:39), still there, fresh even, able to be examined, but now painless, a token not of a past horror, but of a passage to a new birth.

For me the physical pain was not even over. I had torn badly at the birth, and had to be sewn up. I was still extremely weak, and I vomited when I drank the champagne that we had packed along with the Kitzinger gadgets in the suitcase. Over the next few days my stitches caused me a lot of trouble. I could not sit on an upright chair, even on top of three pillows. Since hospital regulations said no mother was to have meals in bed after the first day this meant I had to eat standing up. It took up to a full five minutes even to get out of bed, because the slightest movement was so painful. But I was happy, even in this pain. I knew the truth of my first welcoming words to my baby: 'It's all right'. (Later I learnt that Peter Berger had called this common message of comfort from a mother to her child a metaphysical statement.)

If my first words to Dominic were 'It's all right', Peter welcomed him with an even more explicit promise of the ultimate rightness of things. While I was being cleaned up after the birth Peter was given the tiny bundle of blanket and baby to hold. He said he was afraid he might drop it, but he sat down and looked into Dominic's alert little eyes. 'I have something very important to tell you, Dominic', he said, 'the facts are friendly.' These words, familiar to students of the philosophy of religion, were Dominic's first lesson in religious education. They expressed something very important that, as believers, we wanted to hand on to our child. It was a belief that we had just intensely re-experienced in the moment of giving birth.

Childbirth is a peak experience, but not a lying one, not a brief moment of success in a miserable, hopeless world that will soon swallow it up. It is a privileged moment, God-given for our learning, so that remembering what we then saw so clearly our whole lives after may be bathed in light.

6

Looking after a baby

Looking after a baby takes a lot of time, especially if it is your first one. Not that there is anything to do other than feed it, change it, cuddle it and gaze at it, but all these take a long time and have to be done at very frequent intervals, punctuating the night as well as absorbing the day. I took a few books into hospital with me and did not have time to open any of them. Once I was home there were additional baby-related things like nappy buckets and laundry to see to, although free of hospital routine I was at least able to sleep when I wanted to and go back to meals in bed.

I am very glad I was able to be totally and solely concerned with Dominic in his early weeks. I retain printed on my memory the sight of him, lying on the bed next to me, cradled in my arms, sleeping and peaceful. I remember his features, his broad little hands, a pinkish patch on his right cheek that faded after a week or two, his look of Peter. I always want to remember his babyhood, because that is when I first became so close to him, when I was so heady in my love, so easily tipped over into tears if a nurse told me not to do this or not to do that, not to walk around with him in my arms (yes, would you believe hospital regulations?), not to feed him at intervals of less than two hours (many nurses would have disagreed with her). In fact it is normal to have the weeps three or four days after the birth — it is something to do with the descent from the climax of the birth, and nothing to do with the longer-term phenomenon of post-natal depression.

I had no problems with breast-feeding, not even an initial soreness. Dominic and I took to it together very happily, and in fact I did not manage to wean him until half-way through my second pregnancy (and even then he wanted to take it up again a whole year later, when he was practically three). I found it very moving to see my baby drawing food from my own body, clinging happily to my breast in silent absorption. I found it a moment of great intimacy at first, as I marvelled at Dominic's acceptance and enjoyment of me, and I did not like it when the nurses came to see if I was doing it right and to tickle his cheek to keep him sucking. By now I must have fed for hundreds of hours and think nothing of it — I would be bored if I did not have a book or a conversation to keep me occupied — but always at the back is this pleasure in providing, this happiness in an exclusive intimacy between me and my baby.

One of the worst things about looking after little babies is getting up in the night. There is a good side of it, the secret togetherness of mother and child while all the rest of the world is still and sleeping. But this is usually spoilt by the fact that you are so tired. Our sleep goes in waves, and you are lucky if you are caught in a shallow trough, for there is no predicting at what time a baby will wake and cry. Only an hour later you might be at the depth of a pit and then it is very difficult to hold on to the baby as you sit with your head nodding. Hours of sleep can be made up, but a broken pattern of sleep is more difficult. It takes a toll out of every mother until at two or three months the baby is big enough to sleep through. When I had my second child I gave up this getting up in the night business. Instead I had her crib by my bed and just lifted her in to feed when she cried. I put her back again when I next woke, which might be twenty minutes later or two hours later. I was very aware of the little creature even while I slept, and never felt in danger of smothering her.

Another problem is coping with hearing your child cry. Some little babies just cry and cry and you do not know why. Especially if it is the first baby, this worries you, because you want to be the best possible mother and you feel you have failed if for hour after hour, day after day, you cannot bring comfort. Parents work out various ploys to send their babies to sleep: playing Beethoven's Fifth loudly, driving round the ring road at over 50 mph . . . there is even a tape you can buy in the USA of the mother's heartbeat as heard from inside the womb, and I have used this with my babies with fair success. Some say a vacuum cleaner is as good. But there are babies who do not respond to such means, and who cry even though all their physical and emotional needs have been well met. It may be colic. Or perhaps existential Angst. All babies do it a bit, some a lot, and I was lucky that Dominic was fairly average and Cordelia and Benedict fairly exceptionally tranquil — Cordelia even had to be woken for feeds.

It is easy to say: Do not worry, you can do nothing more, plenty of babies have cried like this and they do not show any signs of emotional deprivation when they are older. I think in the end that is the right advice, and if all else has really failed the best thing is to push the baby to the end of the garden where you can't hear it and then to not feel guilty. Unfortunately the neighbours may hear it, and then you will not be able to not feel guilty, which is difficult enough anyway.

Not feeling guilty is possibly even harder today than it used to be, now that there are so many schools of advice, so many idealistic words poured into baby books, such high maternal hopes. But what is most important is to convey to your crying baby the sense of 'It's all right', and you can do this to some extent even if you cannot stop it crying. If you are not worried the baby will pick up your sense of security. Maybe it is in pain, but you can cry from pain and still have a sense of it being all right. Maybe this is why second and subsequent babies tend to be easier than first ones, because the mother has to make them wait sometimes while she attends to the other children and she does not have time to feel guilty about it.

Despite the dangers of guilt it must be recognized that a baby's crying is meant to disturb the mother. It is an in-built mechanism for getting the baby's physical and emotional needs satisfied, and it would be a funny sort of mother who did not wake in the night when her baby cried or feel relieved when it stopped crying and went to sleep. One of the most beautiful things about motherhood is this ability to respond to distress and bring consolation. In fact it is this more than anything that marks out a child's relation with its mother from all its other relationships, and it goes on right through childhood. However involved the father, for example, is with the child, the first and closest bonds of providing and intimacy and comfort are forged with the mother, through the womb and breast at least, even if the nappy-changing and dressing and bathing and taking for walks are shared.

In the end it must be admitted that little babies are rather limited. I adore them, and like to have a peep if a pram goes by, but there is not a lot you can do with them apart from the daily care that must be done anyway. New parents can talk for hours about the way their baby kicks in the bath, or when and how much it vomits, or whether it follows a mobile with its eyes; and new grandparents, just as enthusiastic, have been known to tape-record a full ten minutes of baby-bubbling noises to play to their friends; but much of this zest is concerned with the novelty of having a baby rather than with a special relationship with this particular child. The sign of this is that such keen observation tends to be much more muted the second time round. In Dominic's baby book is recorded the date at which he first sucked his toes, tasted solids, turned from front to back, turned from back to front, sat up supported, sat up unsupported, moved from the baby bath to the big bath, smiled, grasped something in his hand and so on. It was fun watching it all, fun recording it, and I am glad I had the time to do it and the enthusiasm to pinpoint each milestone. But I did not do it with Cordelia and Benedict, and that was not because I loved them less. Indeed I have heard a mother of four rather commend the more relaxed approach to subsequent children: with the first one, she said, you are always anxious about whether it is doing things at the right time. Is it late walking? Is it late talking? Now I am on my fourth, she said, I do not have these worries. I know this one will walk and talk in her own time, because the others all did, and I do not give a fig when it is, early or late.

When new enthusiasm wears off, the one strong thing that remains in early babyhood is the bond being slowly forged between mother and child through sheer physical intimacy. It is symbolized by the picture that has inspired so many artists — a baby feeding at the breast, or sleeping on the breast, full, satisfied and loved. This picture, so rich and evocative of maternal love, is a wonderful image of God's

care for us: the breast unites food, love, warmth and
intimacy with the giver of our life. God our mother, we
believe, gives us our needed nourishment with an equal
love and intimacy.

Whenever we recite the Lord's Prayer we say: 'Give us
this day our daily bread'; we could as easily pray for regular
supplies of milk, the most balanced and complete of all
foods. Whenever we receive nourishment, be it physical
food or spiritual strengthening, we should be aware of God
our mother who produces it. When we say grace before a
meal we can think of God as being as close to us as we eat as
we are to our children when we feed them from our breast.
When we listen to music, or read an inspiring book, or go to
communion, we can think of the warmth and intimacy of
the God from whom this nourishing flows. Jesus spoke of
the 'spring of water welling up to eternal life' (Jn 4:14), but
in much the same way we can think of milk springing from a
mother's breast. The more the child drinks, the more the
mother produces. If a separation prevents the child having
its normal feed, the mother's body still produces for it: the
milk will be made, perhaps overflowing and oozing out. So
is God's love unstinting; if we ignore her, she can never
forget us; her supply of good things for us, of love and
opportunities for growth, does not stop, but is 'good
measure, pressed down, shaken together, running over'
(Lk 6:38). Just as the feeding baby will fall asleep happily on
its mother's breast when it has had its fill, so should we feel
that all the experiences of the day are nourishment in our
human growth, and fall asleep with satisfied trust in the
arms of God each night. Indeed there is a strong tradition of
commending ourselves to God's care as we end each day.

God can be found not only in this idyllic picture, but also
in the times of difficulty, the night wakings, the constant
crying. Just as the human mother cannot sleep while her
baby is crying, so too God is with us when we feel alone or
in darkness, when we suffer from spiritual hunger, from
pain or from fear. Like the human mother she stays with us
through the night hours, even if she cannot comfort us,
holding us in her arms, rocking us, offering us her breast.
While the human mother staggers with tiredness, weeping
or even cursing her disconsolate child, but unable to shut

out its crying that goes on and on and on, God is the mother with no physical or psychological limitations: she is most present of all when we feel totally alone, desolate and inconsolable. How important it is to learn to cry for our mother, knowing that she hears us and cannot rest till we are at peace.

If, despite such a theory, we simply have no sense of God's presence in our times of distress, it might be helpful to think of a similar experience of human babies. Often, in order to help a baby, we have to make it wait while we prepare something for its good. The baby howls, unable to understand why its mother will not comfort it while it is crying for her so hard. Very young babies, for example, may cry piteously when they have their nappies changed; but the mother knows that if she did not change the nappy the child would eventually get a painful rash. Or a baby with a 'sticky eye' infection will howl and struggle frantically to avoid the eye drops that will cure it. Again, a hungry baby just old enough for solids may scream with a strong sense of neglect if the mother puts it down to prepare a feed; but unless she puts it down the hunger is simply prolonged, and she has no way of making the child understand that she is doing all in her power to satisfy its needs as soon as possible. So may we think of God our mother preparing all things for our good. When she seems to bring us pain or discomfort she is strengthening us for future health. When she seems to deny us what we need she is already in the process of preparing something even better, just a little further ahead. When she seems unable to hear us she is merely unable to make us hear or understand how swift will be our relief, and how much worth waiting for. 'All things work together for good' (Rom 8:28), and if the almighty God is indeed our creating, caring mother, how could it not be so?

7

The second birth

My first year as a mother passed happily. We were proud of Dominic and he already fulfilled our desire to be a family. Moreover I had managed to work out a daily regime that gave me enough time to work on my theology (and that was very important to me): I got Dominic to play by himself, in a baby bouncer or in a play pen, for an hour every morning, and in the afternoon I worked for a couple of hours while he slept. It was not a lot and it was often open to interruption, but I managed to research and write a short book — my first — under such circumstances.

What made us disturb this satisfactory set-up was the wish to have children close enough in age to play well together. I had admired families where the children were real playmates, and wanted to vary the pattern of my own childhood where a brother, older than me by three years, had rarely shared games unless we were brought together by my father's imaginative organization. The combination of different sexes, a three-year gap, and perhaps a degree of temperamental difference had separated us. The only one of these factors I had any control over in the case of my own children was the spacing of the births, and so I was keen not to delay over the second child. Shortly after Dominic's first birthday, I became pregnant.

Pregnancy was a good time, as it had been before. But this time I spent less time simply relishing my state, and sending waves of tentative love towards the being inside me. I was busy with Dominic, and I was also fulfilled with him. The first time I had desired a baby with a longing that dominated all else. This time I could perfectly well do without one, at least for the time being, and so, although I sometimes thought of my unborn child with love of our intimacy, I often forgot it, I let it slip from my mind. And so the pregnancy quickly passed.

The birth was not only happy but dramatic. In fact it resulted in a radio interview for a small local station, and a story and photo of myself and the child splashed over the front page of one of our more downmarket local papers. They were short of news that week. 'Meet the mum in a million!' it read. And again 'Margaret's tiny bundle of joy', 'Supermum Margaret cradling her two-day old baby daughter'. The only bit we objected to was when Peter was reported as having said 'The little baby is beautiful'. He protests he said nothing of the kind, and would never have said anything so banal. In fact his only comment on that subject was 'I hope her looks improve'. But I have no doubt that she was beautiful from the first.

What had happened was this. The onset of labour had been as blurred at the edges as it had been before, with isolated contractions waking me in the night for a whole week beforehand. Then one Sunday morning I started a regular sequence of very light contractions. I thought it best not to drive the car, in case I got stuck, but I did not want to miss mass. I rang up some friends and arranged a lift. In the middle of mass the contractions stopped.

I talked on the phone to a friend about it — a mother of four. She remembered the awful fuss over the birth of her second child, when early light contractions were mistaken for the real thing, and she ended up with a two-day 'labour' with fussing midwives, doses of castor oil, and a resulting state of total exhaustion. She said 'When you really get going, it is so unmistakable'. I thought back to my first birth and agreed. When you really get going it is quite unmistakable. I determined not to get alarmed too soon.

Towards the end of the afternoon the light contractions started again. I rested in the garden on a sun lounger, talking to Peter while Dominic played. After I had put Dominic to bed and eaten some dinner I went to bed myself. I practised some relaxation exercises in the dark. Probably as a result of these the contractions became stronger. I realized I had come to the 'unmistakable' stage, but it had come at a very inconvenient time. I was tired and had had no sleep. Moreover I could not face the idea of having people around

me who were tired and who had had no sleep. I did not
know whether to call the midwife or not. I went downstairs to Peter who was watching television. He said he was
so tired he could not stay awake. He urged a short sleep
before ringing, to set us up for the testing time ahead.
Though divided in my mind I agreed.

I could not sleep, but I had learnt to relax fairly well, and
it is extraordinary how refreshing this is. I could not time
my contractions in the dark, so I counted them instead.
After about ten I went downstairs to ring the hospital. I
thought I would let Peter sleep till the midwife came. I
knew the first thing I would be asked was how frequent the
contractions were, so I tried to time the interval between
one and the next. While I was doing this I was delayed again
by a desperate need to go to the loo. Normally a midwife
gives you a suppository to clear out your bowels, but this
time nature took its course without need of such devices.
The contractions were very strong now, and I kept having
to stop half-way across a room to cope with them.

Coping meant a combination of relaxation, breathing
technique and focused concentration. Once you have
learnt the breathing it comes naturally and helps a lot; I do
not know why it works but it does. The relaxation is closely
tied in with it. The point of focused concentration is to
provide a counter distraction, and for my object of concentration I had chosen to run mentally through the Lord's
Prayer. I think this helped me a great deal to keep on top of
what would otherwise have been excruciating pain, and it
is some measure of how strong the contractions were that I
had difficulty in stumbling through the words in the right
order. I found one contraction took me twice through the
prayer, so I also had a measure of my progress towards the
moment of relief. The worse the contractions were the
more I found myself not just saying the prayer, but praying
it. Acceptance of suffering and plea for help are so mingled
there that no prayer could have felt more suitable. 'Deliver
us from evil . . . deliver us from evil . . . ' but 'Thy will be
done'.

Even after I had eventually staggered to the phone and
lain down next to it on the sofa there were more delays. On
the other end of the line the hospital nurse kept on asking

questions, that seemed so daft when I was having difficulty speaking and all I needed was a midwife and that quickly. Full name, expected date of delivery, name of doctor, any previous children, expected length of stay in hospital . . . . I really do not remember what she asked, but it seemed to go on for an awfully long time. She told me to stay by the phone and the midwife would ring me back. There was perhaps a quarter of an hour's wait — later I learnt the midwife had got the number wrong and this had held her up.

By the time she rang I could hardly speak. Between the end of one contraction and the beginning of the next there seemed to be time to stutter out two or three words only before I was overtaken by a desperate need to 'breathe'. The midwife — whom I had not met before, my regular one having the night off — kept on saying I had better get to the hospital as soon as possible. I knew it was too late to move, and anyway since Peter did not drive I could not go unless the midwife drove me or ordered an ambulance. I could not say any of this. Every sentence I started got interrupted and unfinished. Suddenly I felt a new sensation, a sort of violent wrenching that moved the contraction down lower. I knew it meant the baby was on the way out, but I could not believe it had happened so soon. I thought I had an hour or two still in hand. I managed to blurt out 'I think I'm going into the second stage' and at last the midwife stopped going on about hurrying to hospital. She said 'Put down the phone and I will be with you as soon as possible'.

A wrench or two later and I put my hand down between my legs. There was a soft warm bulge emerging that could only be the baby's head. 'Weren't you frightened?' people asked afterwards. I had not time to be frightened. I thought 'I just have to hope the cord isn't caught round the neck. As long as it isn't, it will breathe. And if it breathes, that is all there is to it.' I caught my child as she hurtled out, all warm and wet and slippery, and turned her over to see her sex. When I saw she was a girl I felt happy and relieved. She breathed at once, in tiny little cries. I thought I should tilt her mouth down to drain it, and maybe clear it out with a finger, but when I did this she cried. She cleared her breathing better by her own efforts.

I held the little baby against me, and we sat in silence.

Between my legs was a pool of blood and water, and I knew if I got up it would fall all over the white rug by the sofa. So I just sat in the silence of the night with my new child in my arms and wondered if it was true. Was it true that my labour was over so soon, that that pain was already finished? Was it true that I held a child in my arms, that I had delivered without the help of any other person? Was it not possible that this was some sort of hallucination brought on by the labour? People can behave very strangely in labour. I held my baby and looked at her and loved her and at the same time disbelieved in her. I was wearing a thin kimono dressing-gown, half-open, and by now sodden. The baby was covered in creamy vernix and her hair looked dark in its dampness, a shade darker and thicker than Dominic's. Her chin and hands were thinner and more delicate than his had been. All the time the cord was still there, joining her to the inside of me from where she had come.

After some minutes I realized she was beginning to shiver. Though it was midsummer, it was after all the middle of the night, around 2 a.m. Still holding her I stood up, and the pool of muck fell with a thud on to the rug. I hobbled to the door, opened it, and called quietly, for fear of waking Dominic, 'Darling!' Peter woke at once and called back without hesitation 'OK, I'm coming'. I went back to the sofa with Anna Cordelia (for so we had decided to call her) and sat down. When Peter came in he looked blankly at us, not comprehending. I said 'It's a girl'. I said, 'She is getting cold, can you get a towel to wrap her in?'

After we had wrapped her up we began to rejoice together and believe in what we saw, since we both saw it. When we heard the midwife's car arrive Peter went out light-heartedly and proudly to greet her with 'Come and see this little girl'. She showed no surprise when she came in, and set about her tasks in a coolly matter-of-fact way. I had, after all, given her a fair bit of mess to clear up as a result of my tardiness in calling her. She had also, she told me, had only an hour's sleep after the last delivery, and had an induction to do at 8.00 that coming morning.

She injected me, delivered the placenta, cut the cord, inspected my tear and pronounced it pretty bad (it is extra-ordinary the way you do not even know if you have torn:

the other sensations are so powerful that even ripping flesh passes completely unnoticed). Then she rang the doctor and her pupil and arranged for them to come with the necessary materials to sew me up. I had said I did not want to go into hospital and although the midwife said 'We shall have to see about that', I heard her take my part on the phone against the doctor who seemed to prefer to stay in bed.

The next two or three hours were happy and busy. The doctor, once he had properly woken up, was his usual jokey self, and the pupil midwife was delighted with the aesthetics of the home delivery and wondered why I had ever planned to go into hospital. Even the midwife thawed and did a magnificent job of washing all the stains out of the rug and my kimono and the baby's towel, before leaving only a couple of hours before her next job. Her last words as she left us all tucked up in a row, Peter, then me, then Anna Cordelia in her crib, were 'Do you want the baby in bed with you?' 'Not tonight', I said, feeling this was the right sort of atmosphere for having a baby.

Only the baby slept, as we waited for Dominic's inevitable waking. He was right on his usual time, and Peter brought him and showed him the little figure in the crib. He was so excited that we had to hold him back from straight away picking her up and cuddling her in his little arms. 'This is Anna Cordelia', Peter said, 'She is going to live with us for always.'

Over the next few days the congratulations poured in. I could not have been more happy with the way things had worked out. The labour had been less painful than before and taken me by surprise with its brevity. The alienating features of hospital supervision had been avoided, and the whole of this intimate event had taken place where it seemed rightly to belong, in the home and among the family. Most important of all, I had a lovely daughter. I felt I knew her well, right from the start. I felt I could see in her face that she was the sort of person one can only describe as very good-hearted. Nothing in later experience has caused me to question this first judgement.

Disbelief was the most striking characteristic of this birth. I had felt disbelief the first time round, when only the sight of Dominic could convince me I was capable of producing a real, lovely human baby that I could love without reservation. The second birth had much of that with a new dimension besides — the experience of sitting alone in the night with my baby in my arms and not knowing if she was real; the experience of not trusting the evidence of my senses without confirmation from others, of not daring to feel the joy that bubbled up within me for fear of deception. The peak moment that I had experienced at the first birth had been in one sense definitive: if I could produce one marvellous baby I could produce two; if I could welcome one child with joy and love into the family I could welcome two. Yet the same doubts came back — could something so wonderful happen to *me*? — doubts that I barely admitted, and yet so deep that they resisted even the evidence of my eyes, until I had confirmation from others.

Peak experiences, revelations, visions — whatever we choose to call these experiences in which we are surprised by joy — all seem to have this dual quality of definitiveness and repeatability. What we see in our privileged moment is true for all time, and yet if we see it again we are surprised again, because we can never trust completely in our memory. The happiness of that vision is not lessened by being repeated, its freshness does not pall with familiarity. We learn, perhaps, something about the unimaginable experience of heaven. An eternity of vision, in which every moment is as fresh and surprising and joyful as the last, because if it were to fade for an instant we would stop believing that it had happened. A community of loving, in which the presence of others enables us to rejoice, because without them we would fear we were hallucinating. The joy that a mother and father feel constantly reverberating off each other as they look at their children and then at each other and then back at their children, marvelling the more because the other marvels too: this will be multiplied a million times over in heaven, where the hosts of saints and angels rejoice to join their voices in an unending hymn of praise, rejoice to share a vision which, as often as it is echoed in another's joy, is increased like a beam of light, reflected in a million mirrors.

8

A crisis in mothering

Only a few days after the birth of Cordelia I began to have some sense of what I had let myself in for. Dominic was obviously proud of his sister and excited by her arrival — he learnt to kiss for the first time in order to kiss her, and he struggled to be allowed to hold her in his arms, his face shining with defiantly independent delight. But he was too little to hold her successfully, and she always cried. Angry with this rejection, he hit her in the face. This happened for the first time perhaps two or three days after her birth, and was to be the pattern for the next eight or nine months.

Three weeks after the birth, the Pope died. From our point of view it was an exceedingly ill-timed death, even if from Pope Paul VI's point of view it was a beautiful moment — the Feast of the Transfiguration. Within a few days Peter was dispatched to Rome to cover events for the press, and we did not know when he would return — it depended on how long the conclave lasted. Baby in, Daddy out, was not a happy combination for a child less than two years old who understood practically nothing. He did not openly grieve, but he developed a hard little shell of defiance with which to cope with the disappearance of his father, the rejection by his new sister, and the ineffectual attempts of his mother to sow harmony with an air of calm patience.

Peter came back, with some very welcome earnings, and we tried together to convey to Dominic a sense of patient understanding, with particular time and attention devoted to him, and his baby sister left very much on the sidelines. It was not a good policy, though it was the sort of approach suggested by the popular child psychology prevalent at the time. Dominic seemed to feel liberated by the air of tolerant understanding to step up his attacks on Cordelia, and his provocation of his parents.

Four weeks later the Pope died again. This time, I thought, let us all go. The first time it would have been out of the question because the baby was so young. This time the baby was old enough to travel while small enough to be easy to look after; we felt we were earning enough out of the work to be able to afford the extravagance; I had been disappointed to miss the last event and had promised myself to go the next time — not of course dreaming it would be so soon; and, decisively, we thought it would be better for Dominic.

It was rather a disaster. Our carefully planned hotel booking — phoned and confirmed with a reply-paid tele-gram — fell through, so that instead of the two rooms we had asked for in a hotel with good telephone facilities, we got stuck in one tiny room in a small pensione where the chamber maid stole £200 from us and Peter had nowhere to write his stories. Dominic and I became increasingly under-slept, and babysitters were only to be found for the evenings and not, as we had hoped, for the mornings too. The skycots we had carefully ordered for both flights failed to turn up, and Cordelia returned home with a red swollen eye where Dominic had scratched her in the aeroplane.

Back home Dominic's behaviour became more and more intolerable. I was heartbroken that my attempt to give my beloved child a sibling had backfired so painfully. Once I had a child I was delighted in and was proud of. Now, instead of two such children, everything had gone sour. I dared not enjoy my little baby for fear of making Dominic jealous, so she just about got her minimum number of feeds and for the rest had to cope for herself. Meanwhile the child I had once thought so lovely had turned into a monster. He wore me down with his violence and defiance, and I wondered how I had ever managed to like him. 'I ought to be enjoying him so much', I thought, 'This is meant to be the happy time you look back on, that passes so quickly.' Feelings of failure and guilt merged with those of dis-appointment and disillusion. I grew to hate children.

There was not really any area in which Dominic and I could live together in harmony. I would awake each morning to the sound of Cordelia crying — not because she was hungry, but because Dominic had begun the day with hitting her. If I did not respond at once Dominic would make quite sure I knew by crying out 'I hit baba'. I wondered why, with all the child safety aids available on the market, no one had invented a cradle on a pulley that could be hauled up to the ceiling: I could find nowhere to put the baby that was safe from Dominic, and I feared that if I locked her in a room on her own she would be deprived of stimulation and company, and I would not hear her when she cried. Usually Dominic's attacks were with his hands, but once I caught him just before he hit her with a bread knife, and another time with a metal car.

When Dominic eventually grew tired of hitting Cordelia in the mornings he discovered a new way of beginning the day: he would take off his nappy and shit in the middle of the floor; then he wiped it all over his cot and the rest of the furniture. It took an hour to clean up, and of course while I was doing this he would be setting about creating havoc somewhere else. His favourite game with his toys was to take them all off the shelves and throw them round the room, so that he could see me go round picking them all up. Several times when he had a bath I discovered him emptying buckets of water on to the bathroom carpet. Bathing the baby is supposed to be one of the little tasks in which the toddler can feel happily involved, but it was never that way with us. Dominic would wait until I was holding Cordelia carefully in her baby-bath, and then throw into the water everything he could lay hands on — talc, nappies, her clean vest and nightie, tins of cream and bottles of baby lotion, pins, tissues and hair brush. While I was busy fishing them out Cordelia got cold, and we would end the bath with everyone in tears. I took to bathing her not more than once a fortnight, as I never found a way of solving this problem.

Every treat I tried to give him, at least to provide some temporary distraction, ended in disaster. If other little children came to play he would go up to them and push them over so they landed on the back of their heads, and when they got up he did it again; so even the attempt to get together with other mothers suffering the same two-year-old difficulties was too exhausting to be worth it. If I organized an outing to somewhere like the zoo there would be such tears and struggling when it was time to go home that it seemed almost unkind to have taken him in the first place. Even when we went shopping — which we had to almost daily — he would pull the goods off the shelves, and once I had literally to put my foot on him as he wriggled on the ground, because I needed both my hands to get out my purse and pay so that we could beat as speedy a retreat as possible. Public scenes like this are indescribably painful and humiliating: you naturally think you would never let yourself get into that situation, and then when it happens to you you do not know where to look or how to cope with your shame.

Possibly the most hurtful thing of all was the exclusion from adult company. Dominic was too disruptive to be taken into any adult gathering, and I have described how even a cup of coffee with another mother and child was virtually impossible — not that talking over the same tiresome problems would have been particularly stimulating or liberating anyway. And yet I was unable to leave him with anybody else. It was not just that I dreaded to inflict him on others' generosity but that he would not permit me out of his sight. After a few months it became clear that I badly needed some escape, and I tried hard to organize a few hours to myself each week. I interviewed a large number of people for a post of child minder, thinking, almost certainly wrongly, that it would be more secure for him to stay in his own home, even though this meant paying appreciably more. I chose a woman who had some experience of difficult children, having had a spastic son herself, and yet a few weeks after she had started Dominic decided he was not going to let her into the house or me out of it. He would throw himself on the ground screaming and beating his head on the floor, until he went red in the face. When I tried ignoring this and leaving the house in any case, ringing from town to see if all was quiet now, my child minder said 'Thank God you've phoned. I've been so worried, I thought he was going to have a fit', and I had to come home straight away. Tied to my child in this way, shunned as he was shunned, I came to be viewed as Dominic's appendage, and no longer an individual in my own right. I began to understand what it felt like to be a leper, and to be — however gently, however understandingly — excluded from the company you long to share. When people spoke to me kindly about the need to endure this difficult period with patience, the tears lolloped down my face.

Six months after the new birth Dominic got whooping cough. Although I took him to the doctor three times over the next six weeks to insist there was something wrong, it was not diagnosed or even suspected until I rang the surgery to announce that he at last had begun to whoop. The six weeks of clingy, mopey behaviour without an explanation had left me even more exasperated, and now we were isolated more rigorously than ever for a few more weeks, forbidden either to receive visitors or to leave the house. The baby naturally caught the disease — barely out of the particularly dangerous period of the first six months of life — but fortunately both attacks were relatively mild. I had decided against the whooping cough inoculation after a careful study of the arguments pro and con, and despite the trouble it brought us I do not regret that decision.

Where I do think I was mistaken was in my general approach of patience and self-sacrifice. I was far too much influenced by the ideology of a child's need for security. I now believe that, unless there are very exceptional circumstances, it is natural for a mother to give all the necessary ingredients of security and caring without needing special exhortation. Security and caring are crucial, but an overemphasis on these qualities in the case of a normally loving mother can lead to a distortion: the child pushes its mother further and further to see how much it can get away with. When Dominic did this to me I was afraid to vent my rage on him, and so I let it destroy me instead. Of course, destroying me, it destroyed both of us. Once I ran into the street and screamed as loud as I could, in the middle of a crowd of people; then I went back home a little calmer. Another time I ran away, leaving the children with Peter: after half an hour sitting by the river feeling guilty and not knowing what to do next I went back. One day I endured all with patience until a shout broke out from me so loud that I lost my voice for the whole of the next day. Even a year or so after the worst of the crisis there were days when, despite my embarrassment, I wept openly in the streets. None of these incidents should have happened, and yet what could I do? There was no way I knew of controlling Dominic, except by locking him out in the garden and hearing him cry and beat his fists on the door, observed by the neighbours, or by strapping him in his cot. I knew that mothers that locked their children in cages got reported to the NSPCC and were condemned by society as inhuman beasts, and yet it often seemed to me as though it would be the kindest, calmest course. If I had had a different upbringing and seen violence in my childhood I would no doubt have battered my children. I am not surprised it is so common.

Eventually my health visitor referred us to a child guidance officer. When I went to the child clinic the sight of all those other little terrors toddling about the floor made me feel so ill that I burst into tears, and when this happened for the second time running the health visitor decided I needed help. In due course Blossom arrived at our house. It was not her real name, but it was the name Dominic always used for her. Blossom had one good effect: she united the family in disliking her. Peter and I disliked her because we thought she was insipid and inexperienced. Dominic disliked her because we spent the whole time while she was there discussing how awful he was. Cordelia was too young to have an opinion.

Dominic set about a systematic baiting of this new visitor that was not without success, and for once Peter and I were secretly proud and delighted. On her first visit Dominic tried to take her shoe off. 'Don't take my shoe off', she said. 'Why not?' said Dominic. 'Because it is keeping my foot warm', she said. 'But it's full of holes', said Dominic. It was indeed a lacey, openwork shoe. Next he climbed on her lap and started to untie her belt. Blossom spent most of the first session trying to keep her clothes on.

After that Dominic and I saw her alone. Dominic's next ploy was to unpack her handbag. He got quite far before she noticed and she was annoyed. She tried to give me an example of firmness by repacking her things and telling him not to do it, instead of removing it from harm's way. Dominic repeated his attack, and by the end of the hour she was obviously tense and irritated, while trying to put on an air of calm control.

In the third session Dominic exposed himself. According to family legend, which is not *quite* true but captures the flavour, he finally demolished her with the challenge 'Have you got a penis, Blossom?' In fact by the end of this session I had had enough of her and told her not to come back. She insisted on ringing a few weeks later to see how we were getting on. I answered the phone cheerily and said everything was lovely. That got rid of her for good, and to this day she probably thinks of our case as one of her most rapid and thorough successes.

As to her advice, it was meant to be non-directive, while in fact it had a clear moral undertone of a sort I did not like. 'You and your husband are both very religious, I gather', she said, 'How does that affect your feelings about Dominic?' 'It helps', I said. Blossom looked surprised and immediately changed the subject. I had given the wrong answer — I was meant to say it instilled guilt feelings. But I had probably found more solace than anywhere else in the Christian understanding that we all fail, that my failures in the field where I most wanted to succeed were not only forgivable but to be expected. My confessor was considerably more understanding than Blossom was, and his advice had been 'I do not think you should feel guilty about not being as good a mother as you would like to be'.

Further than that, Blossom pronounced Dominic a perfectly healthy, capable child. No one in fact had ever suggested the contrary. He had had a bit much on his plate all at once, but nothing abnormal. His terrible twos were a bad version of a standard syndrome. There are millions of mothers undergoing what I went through.

In fact, while Blossom was with us, I did decide to change my tactics, though not in a way she advocated. She recommended me to ignore the fact that Dominic was attacking the baby, and just comfort her as though she had fallen over on her own. When I said that was the approach I had been trying to operate so unsuccessfully for so many months she looked irritated. In place of this attempt not to rise to Dominic's provocations I decided on a very different line — I was going to smack him very hard. Up till now I had deliberately avoided this, because I had read in a book of child psychology that you do not teach a child not to hit by hitting it, which sounded persuasive. But my new policy worked where all others had failed. Dominic stopped his attacks on the baby almost at once, and I finally had a means of controlling him when it was really necessary. After a while a threat of a smack was usually all that was needed.

If Dominic's behaviour turned the corner it took me a long time to recover from the hurt done to my personality by the tensions of those months. For two or three years I wanted to escape whenever I saw a child coming. In fact even now I find the company of little children depressing after the first five minutes, so maybe I need even longer to recover fully. If people call me 'supermum' now, I laugh. Little do they know.

Cordelia has naturally had a different upbringing. In fact months of being hit in the face seems to have had rather a good effect on her character, making her spunky and courageous. She has not picked up any idea from me that she is a delicate plant needing lots of protection. By the age of two-and-a-half she was independent and confident, sociable and capable. From her earliest days she has had to cope on her own, and she found no problem in it. My carefully book-learned principles of child care collapsed when I saw such successful results coming out of comparative neglect. In mothering, as in Christianity, we mess things up by striving too earnestly, obeying too literally, working too scrupulously: we cannot replace grace by effort.

9

Continuing difficulties

The worst part of my life as a mother was now past, but there was never again to be a return to the idyllic world in which my time and sympathy were at the exclusive call of a sole child. From now on there was to be a lot of fudging, a lot of compromise, a lot of subordinating the needs of one to the needs of the other. There was also to be the start of a new age in which they sought solace and entertainment in each other rather than in me, and that was after all why I had done it; their rich enjoyment of each other's company began when Cordelia was less than a year, and has never flagged: it is a constant joy to watch. But hanging over the successes of the coming years was a bitter legacy of strain and tension, deriving partly from the ingrained memories of past failures, and partly from the recurring practical pressures that cannot be escaped in the bringing up of little children.

How often mothers speak of this period as the most exhausting time of their lives, and yet how little these words can mean to an outsider. How often mothers repeat themselves, sometimes angrily, sometimes despairingly, stressing the difficulties of their lot, and yet to others they seem ungrateful and incompetent. Have they not been blessed in having children, while infertile couples, who would do anything for this gift, seem the more generous-hearted? What could be more creative and more rewarding than the bringing up of children, and when has any mother regretted those years? Of course it will be tiring, difficult, demanding, but that is so obviously to be expected. Why complain, when you know that any worthwhile activity requires discipline and sacrifice?

People who say things like this just do not understand the

problems. In fact the only people I have met who really have any comprehension of the difficulties are those who have been through it themselves. Many forms of human suffering are self-evidently horrific: we know without going there how unequal we would be to the demands of working in a refugee camp or among the destitute of Calcutta. But the demands of perfectly healthy small children, and your own at that, seem on a quite different level. How could any normal woman be unequal to that challenge, unless she was lacking in maternal feeling?

And yet failure in this area is so common, and it feels all the worse for the fact that it is so difficult to explain to others. A chief reason for the difficulty is that the build-up of frustrations is so dense and rapid that it is impossible afterwards to recall even to your own mind the succession of incidents, let alone to repeat the details of the problem to someone else. You are reduced to making generalized statements of your reactions, rather than being able to communicate the cause of what is wrong. You find yourself saying feebly, 'I cannot cope with them', or 'They make me so angry', and then so often you are answered with a maddening exhortation to patience. Frustration in communication with adults is added to frustration in handling your children.

As an exercise in communication I made notes one day of a not untypical evening with the children, covering scarcely more than two hours. The children are at this time four-and-a-half and two-and-a-half and we are living in Rome. It was an evening that got slightly out of hand, but did not degenerate into total disaster. It is a typical example of the continuing dimension of failure in my regular life as a mother — not an extreme or exceptional time of crisis. There were moments of success among the problems, and thanks to these I finished up only tense and fed up, rather than weeping and screaming.

The account starts at 5.00 p.m., when our regular television programme finishes, and when I give the children their tea. Today I have an idea for a little treat that will accomplish several aims at once. I suggest we go down the hill, and buy a pizza (which is a popular choice of tea, and can be eaten out of the paper while we are out), a new ring for Cordelia (which she dearly wants, and I have promised as soon as possible), and some bread (which we need for breakfast). The idea is eagerly accepted. 'Before we go', I say, pushing my luck a little, 'Cordelia must do a pee-pee.' Success, and I leave her with tights on but no pants or nappy, thinking she will be all right for the next hour until bathtime. Cordelia puts on a rain hat. I point out that it is not raining but she insists. Dominic decides he will take his gun and Cordelia will take hers.

As soon as we leave Dominic asks which shop we will go to first. I think of sticky pizza fingers over the goods in the toy shop so I say 'First the bread shop, then the toy shop, then the pizza shop'. Dominic says no, he wishes first the pizza shop, then the toy shop, then the bread shop. I decide the point is not worth fighting over, so I agree. Cordelia hands me her hat, which I am to carry for the rest of the trip. Now we discuss what kind of pizza to have. I suggest one with cheese or ham, thinking of protein; Dominic says no, he wishes a pizza bianca, which just has a kind of oil on it and is much less nourishing. I point out contrary merits of delicious cheesy or hammy pizzas. He is unmoved. In the shop he has a pizza bianca, and Cordelia asks for a red pizza, which means one with tomato. Clever girl to get the colour right.

Pizzas in hand we approach the toy shop. Before entering I explain to Dominic that I am not going to buy anything for him today. He protests at this unfairness. 'All right', I say, 'you can have something, but it must not cost more than Cordelia's ring, that is 200 lire' (about 10p). I ensure agreement before opening the door. Once inside I show Dominic several toys for 200 lire or less (party whistles, postcards of animals). He rejects them and makes for the swords and masks. I say they cost too much. He turns to a Spider-Man; I say it is too much. He picks out a larger version of the same sort of thing and asks if perhaps this one is cheaper. I say not, and offer him bouncy balls or packs of transfers. He says he does not like them, but fingers a bicycle, muttering 'I wonder how much this costs'. He already has a better bicycle at home. I explain that you cannot buy a bicycle for 200 lire, and repeat the choice of party whistles, postcards, bouncy balls and transfers. He asks for a larger size of bouncy ball. I tell him he cannot have it because it costs 400 lire. He gives in and settles on a smaller bouncy ball for exactly 200 lire. Success. The ring has meanwhile been chosen quickly without fuss. Success. We leave the shop. Once outside Dominic notices he has left his gun inside. The woman seems to have had enough of us already, and says 'Find it yourself'. We find it.

Barely out of the shop for the second time I remember to explain to Dominic that he must not bounce his bouncy ball until we get home. He accepts this. Success. At the corner the children take the path back up the hill. I wait for them, calling 'Wrong way'. A car sweeps in past them giving me a moment's alarm. The children escape being run over and join me. Dominic says 'I've had enough pizza', handing me a piece out of which three bites have been taken. We proceed towards the bread shop. Dominic runs ahead, and turns back suddenly frightened. 'A dog barked at me behind that fence.' The bread shop is immediately beyond the house with the dog. Since I too am alarmed by barking dogs I suggest we cross the road, and then cross back a few steps further on. This is agreed in principle, but Cordelia has a gun in one hand, and a pizza in the other. I have a rain hat in one hand, and a pizza in the other. I say we will have to finish our pizzas first, before we can hold hands in order to cross the road. We stand around chewing. Meanwhile several people walk past the house with the dog without incident. I feel a bit foolish. We edge on cautiously. The dog has disappeared. Half-way past the house we see the bread shop is closed. We turn back.

Half-way up the hill again Dominic sits down for a rest. He also hands me his gun. We wait for Dominic to have his rest. At the door of our flats Cordelia says she wants to press our bell. She cannot reach it. I am by now holding two pizzas, two guns and a rain hat. I am soon also holding Cordelia. Bell pressed, we head for the lift. Dominic says he does not want to get in. I agree to him walking up the stairs, while Cordelia and I get in the lift. Cordelia says she wants to press the button for our floor. She naturally cannot reach that either. I hump her up. Luckily at the top Peter has the door open for us, avoiding another bell-pushing incident. Dominic arrives. We all go in. The children take off their coats and drop them on the floor. I put down the pizzas, two guns and a rain hat. I take off my coat and hang it up. Dominic is now saying 'Mummy, I've lost my bouncy ball'. I find it. I pick up the children's coats and hang them on the special low-height children's coat rack, that looks like a train and is meant to encourage children to hang up their own coats. I say 'You ought to hang up your own coats'. Dominic, annoyed, takes his coat off the train and throws it on the floor. I give him a count of five to put it back, with a threatened smack. He puts it back. Success. I take off my boots. While I am doing this I see Cordelia pulling Dominic's head to the ground by the hair. I disentangle them. Cordelia protests 'Dommy try to eat me'. 'Did you try to eat Cordelia?' I ask Dominic. Answer uncertain.

Aware that Dominic has only had three bites of pizza bianca, I propose some more tea. Dominic says he wants cake. I get down the cake. 'Not that cake.' 'There isn't any other cake.' 'So I want biscuits.' I get down the biscuits. 'Not those biscuits.' 'There aren't any other biscuits.' 'Then I want cake.' I get down the cake for the second time. Cordelia says 'Also me want.' I hand Dominic a piece of cake. He says 'No I want it hot.' I tell him you do not eat cake hot, never ever ever. 'Then I don't want it.' I give Cordelia a slice of cake. Dominic says 'I want some too'. I give him some. 'No, that's too big.' I give a smaller piece. He accepts it. He takes a bite. 'I don't like it.' Cordelia does not eat hers either. They drink Coca-Cola.

I run the bath, which is by now half an hour late. Dominic comes into the bathroom with his bouncy ball. A second later 'Mummy, I've lost my bouncy ball'. I say I will look for it when I have finished running the bath. He accepts this. Success. I undress him. He goes to the loo to pee. As he lifts the seat it falls off and on to the floor with a crash. He cries. I am by now a bit fed up, and I say 'Don't cry, just pee'. He stops crying. Success. He gets into the bath. I ask if he has had a pee. He does not answer. I ask again. He says 'Yes'. Cordelia comes in and announces she has shat in her tights. I look to see if it is true. It is very true. I am very irritated, for several reasons. Firstly, because I should not be irritated with Cordelia for shitting in her tights. Secondly, because I was already irritated before this happened. Thirdly, because we are half an hour late, and a late bed means I get no work done before dinner. Fourthly, because if I had not saved a couple of minutes before we went out by leaving her nappy off she would not have dirtied her tights. Fifthly, and most of all, because every time she wears these tights she seems to manage to get shit on them first day on; her other tights are all either too small or the wrong colour for the clothes that are not in the wash; I had moreover for this reason bought her a second pair of these tights in the right size and colour only two days previously, and it is this new pair that is now so dramatically and rapidly shat upon. What is she to wear tomorrow? I remember putting her in socks a few days ago, and the lady in the supermarket remarking on it, saying, 'I suppose it's not quite so cold for wearing socks now'. All these thoughts run through my irritated mind, and I do my best to express them without giving Cordelia the impression that I am cross with her for not getting to the potty in time.

I clean up Cordelia's bottom, and put her in the bath. I turn to mending the loo seat — not an easy job, and one that I had been putting off for months. The children keep asking me questions, and I say I am too cross to talk, they must talk to each other, and wash themselves tonight. Peter, who has heard raised voices, leaves his work to come in and relieve the tension for a few minutes. I leave the bathroom to take some clothes from the washing machine, including the other pair of tights of the right colour and size, which I hang on a radiator; I take the remaining clothes to hang up on the balcony.

As soon as I am on the balcony I see through the window that Cordelia has got out of the bath. She wanders round the flat looking for me, and eventually joins me on the balcony. She says 'I cold'. It is early February and she is wet and naked. I tell her to get back into the bath. She howls. I tell her to ask Daddy to dry her. She runs off howling. When I come in from the balcony I hear an irritated Peter trying to get rid of a (now dry?) Cordelia, so that he can get on with his work. She comes back to me crying. As I am still fed up I ignore her. After a couple of minutes she stops crying. Success. She turns her attention to the folding bed. Her idea is to get it down and hide behind it. I tell her it is too late for that game, but I am secretly afraid her attempts will make it fall on her, so guilt takes its place beside irritation. Fortunately the bed does not fall.

I dress Cordelia in nappy and pyjamas. She says 'I no want sloop'. Her sloop is a sleep-suit, that keeps her warm when she throws off her bed-clothes in the middle of the night. Cordelia's method of getting out of what she does not want to do is to say 'Daddy says not', or 'Mummy says not', or 'Nuns say not', depending on who she is talking to. Today she makes a mistake, and says to me about her sloop 'Mummy says not'. This relieves the tension momentarily as we both laugh at her slip. While she is laughing I start to get her sloop on. When she notices she wriggles fiercely. I threaten a smack if she does not stop wriggling. She cries but stops wriggling, and soon forgets to cry when I have got her sloop on. Success. I say 'You forgot to wash your face'. She denies it. I get a face cloth to wipe the dirty marks all round the mouth. When I go in the bathroom Dominic is moaning softly because the water has gone cold, and because he has somehow managed to get his hair wet. I say I will be back for him in just a moment. Cordelia's face washed, I get Dominic out of the bath and dry him. He says he wants his hair dried with the hair dryer. I tell him to put on his pyjamas while I fetch it. He does. Success. Cordelia wants her hair dried with the hair dryer. I co-operate, though her hair is not wet. I tell Dominic to come to have his hair dried. He does. He says he wants it hotter. I turn it to hotter. Cordelia wants another go. Dominic meanwhile moves out of range. I call him back for more drying. Cordelia's dolly wants a go. Dominic now says the hair dryer is too hot. I turn it down, and finish drying Dominic's hair while Cordelia tries to unpack the implements from the hair dryer box. I put them back.

I fetch tooth-brushes. Dominic offers no resistance. Success. Cordelia refuses. I say 'Do you want a story?' 'Yes.' 'Then you must have your teeth cleaned.' This works. Dominic chooses a story and I read it. Cordelia delays over choosing hers. Peter turns up at the vital moment and reads her story, and sings the nightly song to Jesus (usually 'Alleluia') which I cannot face tonight. We get them into bed by the count-to-five technique, and turn out the light. I climb on a chair to unscrew the light bulb (a necessary pre-caution these days) and say my final 'Goodnight, God bless', only twenty minutes late.

*

All this really happened in the space of just over two hours. I promise I have not exaggerated, or conflated incidents from different days. The reader will no doubt have already made a few judgements of her or his own about my children's behaviour and my methods of dealing with it. I, and they, cannot escape such judgements. But I should like to add a few conclusions of my own.

Firstly, it should be clear that if I had not written detailed notes immediately afterwards I would never have been able to explain in full detail to anyone else why I had such a difficult time with the children that evening. One or two points remain in the memory — the loo seat falling off, the hassle in the toy shop — and could have been related, but an outsider would have easily thought 'She ought to have been able to cope with that, I am sure I could'. The problem lies in the multiplicity of difficulties without a breathing space.

Secondly, it is easy to see how a few additional factors could have brought about a situation that was truly critical. Imagine that we had none of the moments of success that enabled us to move on to the next stage. Imagine that in addition I had been feeling ill; that we had got to the top of the hill before realizing we had left the gun in the toy shop; that Dominic had not replaced his coat on the train and had to be smacked; that the bed had fallen on Cordelia's head; that Peter had not been at home to help at the vital moment. One is prepared for a certain number of disasters, but if more goes wrong it can be difficult to survive.

Or imagine that I had been living alone with the children, so that I had no one with which to share the tensions of child-minding; I might have been living in cramped accom-modation, where the children had no room to run about inside, and so were even more full of uncontrollable energy and mischief; we might have been in the sort of flat where the children's uneaten cake was dropped on to and soon squashed into the sofa, and where in order to put the children into bed I would have to pack toys and clothes into cardboard boxes to stand on the doormat; I might have been already troubled by financial worries that would have taken from me any ability to be amused and imaginative when faced with childish japes. How could I have coped with such an evening then?

Or, perhaps worst of all, imagine that I had the sort of children that would not sleep. Blessed indeed is the mother whose children go to sleep when they are put to bed, and do not wake up till morning. Without that break, to relax in the evening as a person in your own right and to get a good night's sleep, the spiral of tension builds up in a dangerous fashion, and I do not know how anyone can survive it. We have followed the course of two hours in the company of little children: imagine that extending, hour after hour, day after day, night after night, month after month, year after year. No wonder some mothers become bitter, aggressive and haunted, cynically mocking sweet sentiments on the nobility of motherhood.

No less than three of my contemporaries as mothers had precisely this problem of sleepless children. Each had two children, spaced a couple of years or less apart, of which one had sleeping problems that spread like an infection to the other. Fortunately none had financial or marital worries on top, though tension originating from the children can soon produce tension in all areas of the family. One mother coped with the problem by sleeping not just in a separate room but on a separate floor from her husband: that way he dealt with the several night wakings — each lasting a good half-hour — of the elder child, while she dealt with the night wakings of the baby downstairs. Another wrote to me that for about a year she had had about three hours sleep a night. The third had exactly one hour without her children out of every twenty-four: after that they would wake up, full of energy, and only consent to go to sleep again in their parents' bed — all four of them together. When mothers talk of the hardship of their life, this is the kind of thing they are talking about. But whoever understands that, unless another mother, or occasionally a father?

10

Understanding and support

I have spoken of the ways in which motherhood has gone wrong for me, of the crises that could not be allowed just to get better with time, and of the continuing daily difficulties that spoil and waste and frustrate. These are my problems and my failures, and yet they are every mother's. Some will have had it worse, some will have had it better, but every mother will know what I am talking about.

A mother who is caught up in trouble like this needs understanding from others — not just sympathy, but an informed comprehension of the problems. She also needs practical assistance, preferably before too much harm is done. But perhaps most of all she needs a way of self-understanding that will unite her torn feelings, and form a bridge between the hopes and promises of the past and the disillusion of the present. I believe this way can be found in God our mother.

As far as understanding goes, all that I have said up till now is an attempt towards helping others to understand. I have tried in particular to dispel the myth that all that is needed is a patient sympathy for the child's limitations. Patience and sympathy are precisely the qualities that the mother naturally has — in a far greater quantity than those with no personal involvement who sometimes like to imply that they could do the job better.

The particular danger in the task of mothering is that a mother cannot escape when the situation becomes intolerable. Most people with demanding jobs — nursing the severely handicapped, for example, or supervising a youth club in a difficult area — can go home at night and leave it all behind, and even hand in their notice if they feel they cannot cope any longer. There is no such way out for the mother. If she is lucky she may have a helpful man around enough of the time to give her relief at crucial moments, but the chances are that the crucial moments will be when he is not there, or when he too feels he has had enough. So she needs practical assistance, and not only for her own sake but for her relationship with the child.

There are refuges for battered wives, where in extreme situations they can find a breathing space and feel totally secure. But as yet there are no bolt-holes where mothers can run and leave their children. Perhaps if the social services opened such emergency refuges they would soon find what a need they answered. If there was only somewhere where you could leave the children with no more excuse than that you were feeling desperate, where you knew that they would be in kind and secure hands even if you left them kicking and screaming, that you could run to at any hour of the day or night, as long as you could somehow manage to get there with the children — perhaps even with an emergency taxi service . . . then how much would be saved on battered-baby hospital bills, at the very least. How soon would most mothers return to the refuge, their ammunition exploded, longing to embrace their children in reconciliation, and tearfully thankful to find them happier and calmer than when they had left them in so much tension. As for the few that would not return, better for everyone that they did not.

It would be an extreme measure for any mother to dump her child in a refuge. That is not the practical assistance that she would seek as a matter of course. More basically she needs the finance and opportunity to give her child a regular relationship with another person or group: she needs nursery schools, crèches, au pairs, child minders, good child allowances to make this possible where the state services are lacking. She needs kind aunties and grandmas who will 'take the children any time', but she may also need paid help that she can make use of freely without a sense of indebtedness. Many women will need this and never get it: they simply cannot afford it, and there are limits to what the state can pay for. Nonetheless it should be recognized as a need, and as a society we should go as far as we can to meet it.

The worse your children are the more you dread to impose them on others. At first you cannot believe that your little horrors may be as good as gold with someone else. And so you keep them to yourself and you get worse and so the children get worse, and in the end they are so dreadful no one else can take them away, because they will not leave you till they have healed the raw wounds in their relationship with you.

That is all very right and normal, that unless a child has made a successful relationship with its mother it cannot make a relationship with anyone else. But in order for the mother to make a good relationship with her child she needs time to herself: time to sleep, time to relax, time to pick up the pieces, time to stoke her fires of imagination, time to do other things and express other parts of her being, so that when she views the approach of her child she may respond with unfeigned pleasure.

I did not have paid help with the children until Cordelia was over one and Dominic three, and we went to live in Italy. Before then we had not much money to spare, and we were accustomed to think of child-minding as a luxury rather than a need, and even then as a second best to the constant happy togetherness with parents that we had managed successfully as long as we only had one child. But I reached the point when I said to Peter 'Look, I just cannot do this job any more'. 'What are you going to do about it?' he said. 'When we go to Italy', I said, 'I am going to get a nanny.' 'Oh are you?' he said, but I did, despite initial pessimistic pieces of advice from Italians about never finding anyone suitable. That is to say, I found a girl to come and look after the children four mornings a week and put them to bed for me one evening. My life changed overnight. I was able to live again. For me that meant going to theological classes and lectures, and out of one such course this book took its beginning. I felt more myself again, and could then give of that self to my children when I returned to them. More than that, I saw how much they benefited from the new relationship, how it played its part in enriching their little lives. They looked forward to the girl coming, and learnt something about relating to other people as well as something about Italy and Italian. My error was in leaving it so late, until I was desperate: it took me a long, long time to recover from the over-burdening I had struggled under for the first year of Cordelia's life.

Those who do not have relief in the most difficult times of mothering will pull through eventually in some sense (though the battered babies may not). They will pull through eventually if they can put an end to child-bearing through efficient means of birth control. The children will grow easier as they grow older, and wounds will heal, given time. But the price they will have paid is to have lost one of the most joyful and longed-for parts of human existence, simply ruined by excess.

Enduring in desperation is not what motherhood should be about. It is not the exciting new life the woman welcomed with open arms as she welcomed her newborn. It is not the mothering that the child longs to be given, and that the mother longs to give. 'Mummy, Mummy, Mummy', cries the little one to its mother, more desperately as things grow worse between them. Sometimes at such moments I have fallen on my knees with my child cradled in my arms, each of us weeping, each of us wanting so much the same thing — to be happy in our love — and yet unable to get there. It is not necessary for wounds to be so deep and painful.

> A voice was heard in Ramah,
> wailing and loud lamentation,
> Rachel weeping for her children;
> she refused to be consoled,
> because they were no more (Mt 2:18).

The feelings of a mother whose child is dead go beyond all depths of grief, but every mother shares a little bit in this who feels she has lost a part of her child's life. Those days that should have been so happy together — irrevocably gone, spoiled by resentment and frustration — for these she will grieve, and wish it had been otherwise.

So indeed will the mother grieve who sees not too much but too little of her child — who by force of poverty must leave her child in others' hands, sometimes fearfully, for she can afford nothing but the cheapest, and spend the day at work, when what she wants more than anything is for them to spend the day together. So too will a mother grieve in more extreme circumstances, who by reason of war or imprisonment must lose months or years of her children's lives, and never know how he would have looked, how she would have toddled, how they would have played together. But truly too does the mother grieve who sees too much of her child, whose eyes are dimmed with fatigue, whose ears are deaf with the sound of crying, who is driven to hate what she most loves, to lose what she most has longed for, and who on top of this can barely forgive herself her inadequacy. Can we not, as a society, do something for these women — understand a little more, provide a little more, criticize a little less?

I said earlier that mothers need a way of self-understanding that will unite their torn emotions, and enable them to be reconciled with themselves. I believe that way can be found in a right relationship with God our mother. Just as our children must turn to us for love, forgiveness, encouragement, hope, so we must turn to God. When we are driven to anger we behave like children ourselves, and justify our feelings with bitter words. We call our offspring destructive and disgusting. We say our task is impossible, and our position degrading. We denounce maternal hopes as illusions. We blame everyone and anyone — our children, our husband, our society. We try to stand alone and supreme — a shining example of suffering and wisdom — but we shine instead with tears and the brittle sheen of bitterness.

We need to be able to let those tears go and that bitterness dissolve and find that, after all, maternity is not destroyed, because it is on our mother's breast that we have been weeping. God will understand all, forgive all, share with us in all, and her tenderness will never crack, nor her imagination fail. In her, there will always be new springs of maternal love, that we can always draw from, so long as we turn to them as a child, accepting our human shortcoming and not rejecting her divine limitlessness. Our rage is futile, our failures irrelevant: nothing and no one will ever destroy maternal love.

Our hopes have been so high, and our love once felt it could reach out and embrace any difficulties, overcome any grief. When we have failed, are we to denounce the aims we once advocated, and deny that seed of promise that was born in us with the birth of our child? If we do we will always be bitter, divided within ourselves, angry that what we once believed in fell to pieces around us. When we fail we need to turn to one who has not failed, in whom hope and achievement are perfectly united, in whom motherly love has lived up to its promise. There is a mother who lives up to our hopes, though we are not she. There is a love that cannot be damaged, though we do not possess it.

We have already drunk deeply, more deeply than we know, of that divine love, and have let our children drink of it through us. But it is not ours to give for ever, it does not originate in us. We must turn back, and drink again, like children, trust again, pray again, depend again. Then, strengthened and consoled by our mother, we can be a mother again to our little ones, letting maternity flow through us, not from us but from God. What we have we are given, what we have not we pray for, what we are not we entrust to the one who is. There is but one mother worthy of the name, and in her we find our resting place and our refreshment.

11

Children and death

One of a mother's greatest fears is that her child will die. I had no idea of this before I had Dominic, but it did not take me long to discover it. Three or four days after his birth I was sitting up in bed feeling a little tired and troubled by the fact that he was crying by night and sleeping by day; the health visitor arrived and said 'That's it, I know. If he is crying you think "What's wrong with him?" and if he is asleep you think "Is he still breathing?" ' I soon discovered 'Is he still breathing?' to be one of my most regular thoughts as a mother.

When Dominic was a couple of months old he nearly stopped breathing. In the middle of one night I was woken by the most infinitesimal noise — a sort of faint glug. I was wide awake in no time, unable to go back to sleep. 'Is he all right?' I thought. I padded on to the landing and listened. Silence. I could not go back to bed without checking. I turned on the light. Dominic was lying on his back in a pool of vomit, not breathing. I sat him up and the sick slopped out of his mouth and he howled and howled. He would probably have died if I had not woken.

I was stunned of course, but stunned rather than surprised. Why else would I have woken if I had not been ready for something like this? From then on it seemed quite to be expected that I would pluck back my children several times from the jaws of death. There would be many more occasions — boiling pans nearly knocked over, high balconies nearly fallen off, cars screeching to a halt just in time, lassos untied from necks, fingers yanked back from live plugs. The constant element of each day's child-minding is the attempt to stop your children flirting so resolutely with death.

One learns to live with these fears, and acknowledge them, parent to parent. One mother whom I met said 'There are so many ways every day that a child can kill itself that I am amazed at the number who reach adulthood'. She was sitting on the bank of a stream as she said this, watching her two-year-old's success in managing not to fall down the bank. But now her youngest child is dying of leukaemia. Was she ready for it? As much as one can be, I should think.

I used to hear how parents would 'have a look in at the children' before going to bed themselves. I never knew why, but now I know, because I do it myself. I tip-toe in and listen by their beds until I hear them breathing. Then I come out again, and say to Peter 'They're still breathing'. He does the same. Once we have reassured ourselves that they are still alive, we can enjoy the beauty of their sleeping forms. They sprawl across their beds in wonderful abandon, like baroque angels. They are so totally committed in their sleep, to physicality, to trust, to self-giving, to the wildest depths of insensibility. But they are still alive. Thank God, they are still alive.

Why do I welcome my children when they clamber into our bed each morning? Why should I be glad to see them, when they always come too early, when I always want to go on sleeping, or to have Peter to myself? From relief, to find them still there. From gratitude, that they should have emerged fresh and full of life, from the quasi-death of the night. It is the same when I recover them from a babysitter, or when Peter brings them home from school. Here they are, they did not get run over, they did not crash their heads on the concrete, they did not fall into the fish pond. Each re-finding of my children is a renewal of life, a sort of new birth, a re-experiencing of their givenness. God's gift to me, still given; her protection, still to be trusted.

I see the point of guardian angels. It is more a point for the parents, perhaps, than for the children. Rarely, as a child, did I fear disaster. Being lost, occasionally, or thinking for a second that I was lost — that would make me afraid. But the constant nearness of death was hard to believe in. As a child one takes it for granted that one will live, and one thinks of a guardian angel — if at all — more as an invisible playmate than as the protector from danger that the parent has in mind. Nonetheless most mothers today do not actually believe in guardian angels enough to pray to them. They may be thought of as a beautiful idea, perhaps a pictorial expression of God's care over each of us, but a firm belief in them as separate personalities is not so common. It is to God herself that we turn in begging safe-keeping of our children.

As mothers we need to be able to turn to God with our fears. Every time the children are late or lost or running a temperature of 104° we need to be able to put our trust in someone more powerful than ourselves, and say 'Please God, you love them too. Please let it be all right.' If we are able to trust in God's love it is much easier to survive these cliff-hanging worries. It is such a relief if we are able to commend our little ones into her hands, and know that she loves them even more than we do ourselves, and that she shares all our concern, all of it, as well as having some further cares for them that are beyond us.

But sometimes it does all seem to go wrong, and God's love seems incomprehensible. I have two friends whose babies have died, one at ten weeks, the other at one week. I think back to my babies at one week and I know how flooded with love I was for them as individuals, even after so short a time. I think I would have mourned for them as much at seven days as at seven months or at seven years. At least if they died now they would have achieved something first, but the smaller the achievement the greater the waste.

Those babies who died were real persons, as their mothers knew they were. Let them not be struck off the roll as barely existing, let their names be remembered: Felicity, of ten weeks; Anna, of one week. To all eternity they will exist as human persons, and yet what kind of eternity can we imagine for them? We cannot imagine. We cannot envisage how God can bring to fruition in eternity the personality lost to this world. What did they achieve in this world? Only a message of the existence of love, a love whose size can be measured by the size of the pain that it leaves behind. How can we square this needless pain with the God who is our mother? What can we say more than 'the Lord gave, and the Lord has taken away' (Job 1:21)?

And yet there is something worse even than this quiet

death in a cot. Six days ago, as I write, a six-year-old boy, Alfredo, slipped down a narrow well shaft in Italy. He lived for three-and-a-half days, sunk in slime and dirt, cold and frightened, without ventilation, or food, or drink. All that could be got down to him was a microphone through which he could talk to the rescuers on the surface. So narrow was the opening that only a man of exceptionally skinny and agile build could go down after him; when one brave, thin man reached him he found him so slippery from the slimy mud that all attempts to pull him free failed; the rescuer emerged, bloodied and shocked, and took several days in hospital to recover. Alfredo died. A death of such drawn-out agony, to one so innocent, caught in the bowels of the earth, strains our trust in God. What possible point could be served by an act of such injustice and terror? It is just conceivable that for an adult there might be some process of purification through suffering, but for a child, too young even for its first confession or communion, there seems no way of making sense of such a horror.

The boy's mother, brave and cool-headed in her grief, made a public appeal after her son's death was announced. 'Alfredo was my son and every mother can understand what that meant for me. I would not like his death, his sacrifice, to have been in vain . . . .' She called for the setting up of an emergency centre for rescuing others who might be stranded in similar ways in the future. 'From today on I shall dedicate my entire life to realizing this project. In this way Alfredo will always remain alive for me. I will know it more and more clearly every time we manage to save a human life.'

Alfredo's mother is an impressive woman, and she is right to say that every mother knows what the loss of her son meant to her. I hardly dare think of it for the terror of the thought. When I see her speaking on television I cannot hold back my tears. But there are few who would have been able to turn so soon to the idea of bringing life out of death. It was no slip that she spoke of his 'sacrifice': she used the word again and repeated it in another interview. What does this word 'sacrifice' mean? It means one thing very clearly to me. It reminds me of another sacrifice, in which a son died, expiring slowly and in agony, trapped — not this time in the depths of the earth, but pinned up above it. This other son said, shortly before dying, 'I thirst'. Little Alfredo unwittingly used exactly the same words in his last moments: '*Ho sete*'. Both were innocent, not just in the sense of not deserving such torture, but in the full, pure sense of a childlike spotlessness.

We have become so immune to the death of Jesus. Familiarity has bred indifference in so many ways, and we respond so little to the sight of a crucifix, or a standard turn of phrase invoking the Cross. Theological terms, vivid with meaning for those who first used them, have dulled our minds and made suspect any flickerings of simple human feeling. The death of Jesus no longer makes us sick or angry, terrified or desperate with grief. And yet it was only after such natural responses that the first disciples found their way through to the supernatural meaning of the event. When, by that route, they found the meaning, they were so overwhelmed by it that they went out and proclaimed it to the world. We think we have found the supernatural response, because we have the right words for it: 'sacrifice', 'substitution', 'satisfaction', 'atonement', 'redemption', 'reconciliation'. But these words are empty unless they spring freshly, full of meaning and life and sense, out of an experience of the simple natural emotions of horror and meaninglessness. Alfredo's death has reminded us of these emotions. He has given us a new chance to respond to Jesus' suffering, as we see it mirrored in his own — more than that, united to his own.

But still we want to ask 'why?', and what kind of an answer can possibly be sufficient? Why does God allow mothers to lose their children down holes, to die in slow agony sixty-four metres below the earth? Why did God allow the crucifixion when surely, as Jesus pointed out in his Gethsemane prayers, an omnipotent being ought to be able to think of some other way? 'Abba, Father, all things are possible to thee; remove this cup from me . . . '(Mk 14:36).

Perhaps no answer can satisfy us. But it may help if we remember that when God let Jesus be tortured and killed it was her own son she was sacrificing; there is no threshold of grief that she cannot have known in seeing her innocent and dearly loved child nailed up to die with no means of escape or of anaesthesia. How could she have allowed these unthinkable experiences if it did not have to be this way? Must she not grieve again with us when she sees those terrible hours reflected in any way in our own experience? Must she not long to take our hand and weep with us for the burden of memories that cannot be borne and cannot be forgotten? If any one knows what it feels like to suffer, it must be God, who saw her child die in agony, and had to let it be.

12

The third birth

When we came home from Italy I was pregnant for the third time. Dominic was by now touching his fifth birthday, and Cordelia was three. I read in a book that you should not tell the children before the third month, when it is beginning to show, but we ignored that advice and told them straight away. Dominic screwed up his eyes in a discerning sort of fashion and gazed intently at my tummy, as though he hoped to verify the claim with Superman X-ray vision. Cordelia was pleased but a little disturbed. She went back to being a baby in her play, and then, six months later, well before the birth, she was over it, and all she could say was 'Mummy, I love the baby so much. When will the baby be born?'

I was glad to be having another child. When I had locked myself away in the secrecy of my study and seen on the home pregnancy test the dark circle that meant 'yes', I had fallen on my knees and thanked God. But it was a hard pregnancy, filled from start to finish with that tiredness that usually passes after the first trimester. I needed ten or eleven hours' sleep a day. Since I had to rise at 6.30 to get Dominic to school on time it was difficult to find enough time for my sleep. If you have to cut two or three hours out of every day, where do you cut them from?

The third time round, it was the most frightened pregnancy of all. At first I hardly told anyone I was expecting in case I had made a mistake and was not really pregnant at all. Later on I was afraid of something being wrong with the baby. Perhaps two beautiful, healthy children (one boy, one girl) was my just allowance? I believed that I could grow to love a handicapped child, but if that was the option I would not have chosen to become pregnant again. I knew that I wanted to have another child if it was as lovely as the last one. But I would find it hard not to regret my third pregnancy if the child that came out was not the kind to make others cry 'Oh, how lovely! Aren't you lucky!' How could I feel I was lucky if others were to draw back in discreet silence and pity, not knowing what to say?

I felt this was likely to be my last child, and I wanted to enjoy it to the full. I did not want any residue of unfulfilled hope to linger, but all to be done in beauty and calm and leave memories that I would cherish for always. I bought a new carry cot, I made a delicate hand-sewn baby robe with a Victorian butterfly stitched on it, I asked for a home confinement and made my bedroom as pleasing an environment as I could for the pain of my labour and the vulnerable happiness of the early days' seclusion with my child. Right up to the expected date of delivery I was making pillow-cases, having a basin installed (it was two-and-a-half flights to the bathroom), and simply tidying up piles of unsorted material that had been lying about for the last six months. Practising my breathing and relaxation was, as ever, an important priority, and then there were complicated arrangements, too tedious to mention, to cover the care of the children and the house. I had sheets of paper stuck to the kitchen wall telling everyone exactly what their responsibilities were at each hour of the day. That way I hoped to keep out of the kitchen entirely for a week or more.

The baby was late. I had been in and out of the early stages of labour for ten days, and had had the midwife round six times in vain, before my waters popped soon after I had gone to bed one night, and I knew this time there was no going back. Peter called the midwife, who had just been getting into her nightie, and then he came and sat by the bed and held my two hands.

I lay on my side, very still, and felt great peace as the waves of contractions rolled over me, each a little stronger than the one before, each a little longer. I remembered how the last time I had meditated on the passion of Christ I had felt nothing, nothing, despite expecting to and wanting to, wanting to share something of that lonely agony. Now I was happy to feel pain and know just a fraction of what it felt like to be so tortured. I had had time to make every sort of physical and spiritual preparation, to the best of my ability. I gave myself into my time of suffering, and used the Lord's Prayer during contractions, as I had done before. No one but I knew it, for I said it silently in my soul; only when I came to the intolerable part of labour — the transition stage — when I felt 'anything, but anything, only take this pain away', only then did I find myself catching on syllables with my tongue: 'come', 'day', 'for', 'give'.

But transition is short, and I knew it, and soon the great lump of a baby was pushing down between my legs, where there was really no room for it, stretching out my perineum (where, I later learnt, my old tear-scar neatly unzipped itself), forcing its way out into the world. I was not feeling up to being propped up or observing the birth in a mirror, so I just lay back, waiting to be told, waiting to be shown, still a little afraid of what was coming out of me. Peter said 'A boy', and in no time his greyish-purply, mucky body with its funny-looking, twisty, grey cord was lain on my breast. I held him and looked at him. He looked all right. So this was my third child — a cross between Dominic and Cordelia to look at — this was the being that had drained me of my energy for the last nine months. Unmistakably mine, unmistakably Peter's. I looked at him and he looked all right.

Various people came in and out — pupil midwives digging out clean linen and baby clothes from the children's bedroom where Dominic and Cordelia still lay asleep...a taciturn doctor dragged from his bed for the stitches and the routine examination of the baby, who dourly nodded and murmured 'That's fine' and departed again...my mother, who had lain awake in the spare bedroom downstairs from the first tramp of feet on the stairs, and had heard the first cry, and now came up for a happy peep and to make everyone cups of tea. All the work was done by about four o'clock, and everyone left us, a family now of five, all tucked up in bed in our home. Little Benedict (for so we had chosen to call him) cried in his crib on his own and would not settle, so I said 'It is not fair that he should have to be on his own on his first night' and we welcomed him into our bed where he quietened at once and slept.

Two hours later there was the usual pitter patter of feet and turning of the door knob, and Cordelia came in. I said 'The baby has been born. He's a boy, and he's here in bed with us', and she was entranced. Ten minutes later Dominic came in, and he cried 'Oh, I *knew* it would be a boy', and the two of them sat on my pillow, jostling for a closer position to the baby, and happily arguing about who Benedict liked best.

All that day I felt in excellent health on my bare two hours of sleep, while everyone else, who had not had the benefit of the new mother's natural bonus of energy, staggered around with sunken eyes. I determined that the next days and weeks were to be devoted to looking at Benedict, to enjoying the sight of him and printing it on my mind, so that I would always remember what my youngest looked like when he was very tiny. I did not succeed: despite hours of just looking I have already forgotten what he was like in those first days which are even now as I write only three months ago. At least I have photos as some record, but I wish I could reach back in my memory to hold on to those living traces and keep them always before me. Perhaps it is meant to fade, to slip away into the quicksand of time — a lost vision. I have one or two clear memories of Dominic as a little baby, but the others are all confused. The three blur into each other, and defy recapture.

Towards the end of the second day tiredness hit me, and, with tiredness, love. Peter had already declared Benedict 'the most beautiful of our babies', the midwife had exclaimed over how 'really gorgeous' he was, and now I looked at him for the hundredth time I saw it was true. He was not only mine and all right, he was full of loveliness. As I looked at him I felt myself falling into his love, slipping away from my old life with its handholds of settled affections. Falling in love is a disturbing and an exhausting experience, and as I thought of his loveliness and my luckiness, tears wet my pillow.

There is no greater gift, I thought, that God could have given me than this child. What in all creation is more valuable than one human being? If I were to be given a huge and lovely house in beautiful countryside, a magnificent reputation as a preacher of the gospel, long life and health and admiring friends, what would that be compared to the gift of this one child? Which would I rather choose? In imaginative prospect I would have chosen the other gifts, but now I had seen Benedict the question was just silly. Now I had seen and loved Benedict it was impossible not to choose him over all else in the world, him together with the rest of the family.

Dominic had been, in a sense, needed: we needed a child. Cordelia had been needed — perhaps not straight away, but sometime: Dominic needed a playmate; we wanted a daughter as well as a son. But Benedict was not needed; he was gratuitous. We could have lived quite happily without him; he was pure gift. After my first two lovely children I had the highest standards — anything slightly less good would have been a disappointment, and yet anything equally good was impossible to visualize. But God had chosen to outdo my imaginings, and to give me not just a good gift, but the greatest possible gift. The greatest possible gift, apart from the full attainment of the mysterious notion of salvation.

The months since then have been spent in happiness. The children have adored their baby brother unreservedly from the first, ever since the first day when Cordelia came home from nursery school and skipped up and down, up and down my bedroom, singing 'Hurray, I'm a big sister', and Dominic, when he came home from his school, quite exceptionally did not go straight to the television but climbed the stairs to kiss and gaze at his little sibling. The moments of post-birth naughtiness have been relatively few, the times of shared family contentment long and rich.

Benedict was born in our home, in the midst of the family, and that is where he belongs. We have all had to make an adjustment in our lives for him — some more than others — but what he has given us is a relishing of a new love that is shared more or less equally — really more or less equally — by all of us. Before, we each had three people to love and we loved them. Now, we each have four people to love and we love them.

It is not a recipe for endless childbearing, far from it. We are limited beings and only with the most tender treading did this child come as a fulfilment of what it means to be a family, and not as a disruption as it was the time before. That tender treading was steered by thought and planning and even money, and enclosed within a thousand details of a material nature. But it was also determined by God's grace, without which even the most enlightened arrangements backfire and prove ineffectual. God gave, and gave beyond our hopes, because it was her good pleasure.

13

Homemaking

Our return from Italy was in every sense a home-coming: we came home to England, home to familiar habits and prejudices, and home to our own house. I did not know how much home meant to me before I lived abroad. I had always taken for granted a sense of feeling at home within society, and I had not felt homesick since my parents went on holiday and left me in the care of some friends at the age of eight. But in Italy I felt homesick, and would spend hours going through our Oxford house in imagination, planning decoration, remembering details, putting myself in thought in the place that I missed.

As well as feeling my own mild sense of disorientation while we were in Rome, I also learned more about the refugee problem from one of our best friends who ran the Jesuit Refugee Service. There are now estimated to be sixteen million refugees in the world. Many of them will never again be truly at home again, in their own countries. Many of them are struggling to look after families of young children in squalid refugee camps where people are dying all around them. In some of these camps the survivors have not even the energy to bury the dead. In such extreme circumstances the need for a home must become one of the most violent and insatiable longings imaginable.

Having children makes a home particularly important. When you are just on your own you can put up with a lot of discomfort. You can be at peace going out to preach the gospel like Jesus, or living in a cave like St Benedict if that happens to be your sort of thing. But it would be difficult for any family with young children to live in peace in a cave or constantly camping out.

Babies need warmth and shelter or they will get ill; they

need continuity of place as well as continuity of person or they will feel unsettled and cry; they need space because there is so much necessary gear for them — dozens of nappies and lots of changes of clothing, readily available water for cleaning them up, and ample stocks of cotton wool, tissues and creams; bulky carry cots and baby-baths, play pens and harnesses, baby chairs and pram wheels. One small baby and its appendages can easily take up more room than an adult person, and by the time it is big enough to do without some of the baby gear it is needing even more room because it is dropping toys everywhere and wanting to run up and down all day long. A mother is soon forced into a lot of material concerns about the home, whether she has previously been that type of person or not.

As well as the practical needs there is a psychological point that is equally important. When you have a family you want to provide a place that is your own and that you will all feel happy in together, where you can enjoy the work of the past and plan for the future, where the environment makes you and your children feel comforted and secure and able to grow. There just is no better word to describe what you want than 'home'. An institution could provide the practical facilities, but it does not fill the psychological need because it is not yours and has not grown as an expression of yourself and your husband and your children. Your home is the place that you make, and that makes you.

Making a home is one of the deepest, intrinsic drives of motherhood. Making your house warm and comfortable and friendly is the necessary physical expression of the emotional security that every mother needs to give her child. The first home of every human being is its mother's womb. There is found warmth, security and softness. When we plan a house for our family it is a sort of projected womb, so it is natural to want to provide warm, soft beds and safe electric points and space in which both children and parents feel free to develop.

Having made a home for your family it is then right and natural that you should go on to share it with others. It is very satisfying to share some of your family warmth and security with guests, whether they just drop in for coffee, share a meal, or stay for a week. I know I have drawn strength and comfort from being in other people's houses, particularly before I had a place that I could really call a home of my own, and I like to think that our house can do something of the same for others. Sharing a home is a way of mediating the strength and comfort that we should spread as Christians. And yet I am always feeling 'Have we done enough? Have we entertained enough people, or the right people?' It is at the same time an area of strength and of failure, but perhaps the main thing is to keep it as a constant dimension. We try always to have a spare bed available, and that symbolizes something about wanting to offer a continual welcome even when we do not get round to issuing invitations.

Children, with their time-consuming needs and their breaking-in on every conversation, may seem to provide a barrier to hospitality, but in fact they are an asset. They may eat up the portion of ice cream you are saving for your guest but at least they make for a relaxed atmosphere. Even if they are asleep they leave enough signs of their presence to affect the whole feel of a house. There is something very comforting about signs of childish inhabitation — screwed-up toothpaste tubes without their tops dropped down beside the basin, green plastic wheelbarrows impeding progress down the garden path, bits of string tied on to the loo chain to bring it down to child level, brightly coloured alphabet mugs hung up beside the tasteful adult china. A house is most a home when made by a family, by a creative co-ordination between the parents who plan it, choose it, tidy it and clean it, and the children who mess it, break it, scrawl on it and yet at the same time have called it into being.

There are enormous variations in the way people express themselves in making a home, and that is what gives a home its personal touch. Some people make a lovely home before they have any children; others let it develop in a more spasmodic and disorganized way over a longer period. Some people take a lot of trouble making a home, and then sell it and make another one. Others would not dream of spending so much time and money on their home, but equally they would not dream of changing it for another.

Some people are happy to think of themselves as home-makers; others feel less comfortable with that role, either because an excess of home-making activity bores them, or because they wonder if it is right to be so materialistic.

There is a strain of Christian guilt, which I have suffered from as much as anyone, that makes one hesitant to put too much stress on the physical home. Making your house comfortable and beautiful can cost so much money that you do not like to display how much money you have spent on what may seem like self-indulgence. There is an embarrassment in the face of the manifest poverty of so much of the world: why should I have four bedrooms and fitted carpets when other families larger than my own have to muck in all together in a mud hut? Should I try to make my house as much like a mud hut as possible in solidarity with the poor as an expression of higher values?

There are certainly difficult and conscientious decisions that have to be made — about how big a house to live in and in what area and how much to be spent on furnishing it. In making those decisions we have to be aware of the temptations of extravagance. We have to be aware that the decision almost everyone comes to is the biggest house we can afford in the best area we can afford with the best furnishings we can afford, and that almost everyone thinks at the same time that they have had to scrimp and save to manage the cheapest thing that would be feasible for them. But we have also to be aware that there is no virtue in paying less than we can afford if the balance is not given to charity but rather spent on expensive holidays or clothes or even on a comfortable sense of security won by a hefty credit in the bank. We each have our own taste in what we do with our money, and taste is not to be identified with merit. We do have difficult and conscientious decisions to make, but having made them let us be at peace with ourselves and at the same time respect the decisions made by others.

Once I thought I was keeping my hands clean of such materialist pollution, but now that I have had four homes with my husband, three with my children, I can discourse for hours on the relative advantages of different kinds of floor covering, as seen from the angle of cost, hard-wearingness, warmth, noise, ease of cleaning, aesthetics and suitability for different types of floor surface. Worldliness? Or the concrete stuff of maternal existence? It is easy to be unworldly if you are not the one who is going to have to clean the floor or buy a new carpet in four years' time if you have made an uninformed choice.

We have grown up with a Christianity that has little room for the physical both in terms of human bodies and in terms of places to put them. Our thinkers and guides have for centuries been men without a wife and family, and without a home unless it be a monastery. Yes, if it comes to a monastery we have learnt to find the sacred in it. Monasteries are places that speak to us of God just by us walking around them. But we have not learnt to relate to the sacred in the family home, so that just by walking around the house of a Christian family we can feel we are drinking in draughts of God. We have not dared to think in those terms.

Yet the experience of a home has often been used as a way into understanding our life with God after death. Wordsworth speaks of 'the kindred points of Heaven and Home' (*To a Skylark*), and any mention of our 'eternal home' is immediately understood as referring to heaven, even if the richness of the images is not fully explored. What we do now to create a home on earth is a learning and a longing towards our heavenly home. No earthly home is perfect: too small or too big, too noisy or too draughty, too far from friends or too near to traffic. But we do not need to despise earthly homes because they can never be right; rather we can become aware of and develop through our present experience the great desire within us for the perfect rest of heaven. 'Home': the very word is so evocative. When we speak of our heavenly home it is no empty metaphor but a rich analogy of the experience we long to attain. Of course nobody knows what heaven is like, but if we are to have some kind of background image it may be better to forget about sitting on a cloud with a harp and think instead of what we most love about our own houses.

Heaven will be like getting home after walking miles through the cold and wet and dark during a bus strike, and relaxing in a deep, warm bath with lots of bath foam and strains of Mozart coming through the open door. Heaven will be like waking every morning in your own bed to find your husband warm and safe beside you, and your children healthy and lively, bouncing in to greet you, and knowing that it will always be so. Heaven will be like coming out of hospital, where you did not like the food and did not like the hours, did not like the people and did not like the room, and knowing that now in your own house you can eat what you like when you like, be with the people you like and be surrounded by objects you like, and feeling so relieved about it that you hardly mind any more if you feel ill or not. When we say heaven is our home we mean it will be a place of uninhibited restfulness where nothing has to be done at any precise time, where nothing grates on our consciousness, and where we do not have to think about *doing*, but can simply *be*.

If we are not good at finding God in our homes, this is not something our tradition has never known, but rather something it has forgotten. In the Old Testament the house and the home were sacred places, blessed with the peace of God. Abraham was called by God to sacrifice those things most precious to him, only to find them again in greater abundance: first he must leave his home and his father's house (Gen 12:1), but he is rewarded with a promised land; then he must give up his only child (Gen 22) but for his obedience he has the child restored, with a promise of descendants like the stars of heaven and the sand which is on the seashore. He provides the model for subsequent Jewish salvation history, in which family and home, descendants, house and land, are valued as the most precious gifts of God, the covenant promise of God to his people.

Furthermore, it is through their valuing of the home that the Jews came to a deeper sense of God: the feeling of peace and security and permanence that they found in their own experience of a house led them to find God's presence in a unique way in the house of God. Already in an early tradition from the book of Genesis we find this sense of complementarity between man's house and the Lord's house, as Jacob promises a house for God if God will bring him safely back to his own house: after the Bethel dream he vows

'If God will be with me, and will keep me in this
way that I go, and will give me bread to eat and
clothing to wear, so that I come again to my
father's house in peace, then the Lord shall be
my God, and this stone, which I have set up for a
pillar, shall be God's house . . . '(Gen 28:20–22).

The next stage was for God to be present in the Ark — a
little house, a wandering house, but still complementary to
the tents of the wandering people. When they find new
homes in the promised land, David promises to replace the
Lord's tent by a proper house, and his son Solomon builds
it. Again there is a complementary sense between the
people's dwelling and God's dwelling: it is because David
lives in a house that he thinks to build God a house — 'See
now, I dwell in a house of cedar, but the ark of God dwells
in a tent' (2 Sam 7:2) — and for this intention God replies
with a promise to establish David's house and line for ever
(2 Sam 7:16). Solomon has no sooner finished building the
Lord's house than he builds a new house for himself, and
the two buildings are described as part of the same project
(1 Kings 6 – 9). The material details are as important and
detailed here as they had been in the description of the ark
(Ex 36 – 38). In all these ways human experience is used to
enrich the awareness of God.

When we come to Jesus we find that the house is still
religiously important, in that much of Jesus' ministry was
carried on in private homes. He went often into other
people's homes as a guest and taught there. He regarded
these occasions as an important part of his ministry, and he
resisted criticisms that he should have refused such hospitality: 'the Son of man came eating and drinking, and they
say,"Behold, a glutton and a drunkard, a friend of tax
collectors and sinners!" Yet wisdom is justified by her
deeds' (Mt 11:19).

From the Martha and Mary story (Lk 10:38f.), when Mary
sat at Jesus' feet and listened to his teaching, totally neglect-
ing the preparation of the meal, we can infer that it was his
practice to talk at length in these situations. Luke 14 —
where he is entertained by a ruler of the Pharisees — shows
Jesus using a private home as a setting both for healing and

for telling parables. The Zacchaeus story (Lk 19:5f.) is an instance of conversion taking place within the home. The incident in the house of Simon the Pharisee — when a woman poured ointment over Jesus' feet (Lk 7:36f.) — has Jesus using a house as the scene for the forgiveness of sins: 'And he said to her, "Your sins are forgiven . . . . Your faith has saved you; go in peace" '. Most notably of all, the Last Supper (following Jewish precedent) took place in a house, and there could be no more sacred moment in Jesus' ministry than that. The most holy sacrament of the eucharist was instituted not in the temple or on a holy mountain, but in an ordinary house.

When in turn the first apostles set out, their base in each town was a private house, and they were urged to make a stable relationship with that home, turning down other offers of hospitality ('And whatever town or village you enter, find out who is worthy in it, and stay with him until you depart': Mt 10:11). More than that, private homes were the first places of Christian worship: it was for a long time the norm that people should gather for the eucharist and prayer in a room of a family house. At this date the ordinary home must have felt a naturally sacred place: religious institutions and churches had not yet had the chance to draw off supernatural functions that found their first Christian expression amid the natural sacredness of home life.

When the apostles left a house, they blessed it with the gift of peace, and that, more than anything else, is the quality that rightly belongs to a home. If all is well, our domestic houses have their own distinct atmosphere of peace and security. It is a fruit of the Spirit, a gift of God, and something to be savoured and recognized as such. It is God's gift to us, her presence in the heart of our home, and her invitation to find her and acknowledge her where she has left her mark. Every house can be a house of God.

Christmas for the mother

There is no time in the Christian year when the home is more important than at Christmas. Christmas is the time to adorn your house, fill it with the food of celebration, and invite those who are alone to come in and share it with you.

Young people who have spent the rest of the year trying to escape their families somehow find when it comes to Christmas that they want to go home. Even those who make a point of going out to share Christmas with tramps or with the sick are spurred by the will to bring home cheer to the homeless: they know it is the worst day in the year to be alone or out in the cold. No doubt it is because the place where a new-born baby belongs is at home. A stable had to do once, but it is not where anyone would choose, and as we remember Jesus' birth year after year we prepare our homes for him as we prepare our hearts for him.

No religious feast requires more physical work. Advent is supposed to be a time of meditation and penance, but usually the mother's mortifications are more worldly and more directly linked to the coming celebrations. If she has time she will profit also from prayer and the sacraments, but this may be the one period when spiritual preparation is cut down to a minimum by the simply enormous number of urgent things to do.

I do not think this is necessarily the overtaking of a religious event by 'commercialism'. If Christmas means nothing to the mother she will bother less about celebrating it, and many mothers do curse the approach of Christmas as a drag. There are those who enjoy Christmas as merely a winter family festival, and elaborate preparations can be a sign of cosy self-indulgence. But they can also be a sign that the mystery of the nativity really means a lot to us. We simply have to examine our conscience on this year by year, though we may remember that we are told in the gospels not to be scrupulous about feasting and drinking when Jesus is with us: 'Can the wedding guests mourn as long as the bridegroom is with them?' (Mt 9:15).

Celebrating Christmas can involve a phenomenal amount of work: there is the careful choosing and writing and addressing and stamping and posting of piles of Christmas cards; the mixing and stirring and leaving and stirring (and wishing) of the mincemeat; the baking and marzipanning and icing and decorating and leaving-to-mature of the cake; the inviting of relatives and friends and the planning of meals and beds and presents; the applying for tickets for a carol concert; the singing of carols in a group for charity; the drawing up and crossing off of lists; the difficult thinking up of suitable presents; the frustrating rushing around the shops on afternoon after afternoon to find exactly what has been chosen; the sweating in over-crowded shops and the shivering outside in the bus queue; the aching arms from carrying heavy loads of shopping; the ferrying home of plentiful supplies of booze; the ordering in time of a turkey large enough to produce satiety but not nausea; the saving and budgeting and inevitable alarm despite all at how much it costs; the taking of the children to see Father Christmas in a big store at a time when you will not find the notice 'Gone to feed the reindeer'; the organiz-ing of child minders while the shopping and cooking is done; the boiling and boiling and boiling of the pudding to make it go black; the remembering to find sixpences or tenpenny bits and the hiding of them where the children will not find them in the kitchen; the making sure that every child has a stocking to hang up without a last-minute rush at Christmas Eve bedtime; the stockpiling of presents on the tops of wardrobes or under lock and key; the getting down from the loft of cribs and fading decorations; the arranging of a car to pick up a Christmas tree; the decking and adorning of tree and pictures and walls and front door; the buying and hanging up of holly and mistletoe and not forgetting to have time for a quick kiss under the latter; the clearing of a shelf or a table for the crib, and the trying to make it even prettier than last year; the finding of a box of crackers that has at least one each but not too many over and still at a reasonable price; the hoping that this household will somehow escape the usual round of coughs and colds; the remembering despite everything else to give something or do something for someone in need; the staying up late to make the mince pies one night, wrap up the children's presents another, and make brandy butter a third; the countdown to midnight when there is the first Christmas mass or service which many mothers still want to get to despite their total exhaustion and their early rise in the morning, when they will have to put in the turkey and attend to their children's bubbling excitement at Father Christmas's visit to their stockings, if indeed Father (or Mother) Christmas has not, horrors! forgotten. All these things are indeed an advent penance of a real, physical, human kind; they are the way mothers put themselves out to show the importance of Jesus' coming in their lives; the way also in which they spread the good news to all — to those to whom they have sent cards, to those to whom they have sung carols, to those to whom they have made a donation, to those who pass their house and see their Christmas tree lit up in the window, to those who share in the turkey they have cooked and the cake they have made, and most of all to their children for whom more than anyone the work has been done, because the whole of the festivities is a huge educational aid for the simple but life-changing message 'Jesus Christ is born'. At Christmas, mothers take the lead in preaching the gospel.

There is a very good reason why this should be so (apart from the less good ones connected with traditional sex roles). Mothers know better than anyone else what the birth of a baby is like and what feelings it arouses. For them the Christ child is not the pale pink plaster doll of the crib, holding out its arms in welcome with the mature muscle-control of a ten-year-old: he is a wet, reddish, smeary new-born, with his cord-stump still on and with huge-looking testicles, howling and hardly knowing how to wave his arms in protest — a sight to a mother of total and tearful beauty. As she once cried out in her heart to her own baby, so she now cries out in her heart to Jesus, 'You are beautiful, you are alive, and you are mine'. Ours, because he is the child born to us ('For to us a child is born, to us a son is given': Is 9:6), the Son of Man. Ours, because he is also our elder brother who gives us a model to follow ('the first-born among many brethren': Rom 8:29). Ours too, because he makes known God our mother to us, that we may know 'that thou hast sent me and hast loved them even as thou hast loved me' (Jn 17:23). Son, brother and parent, Jesus is born into relationship with all of us.

If a mother can better visualize the new-born Jesus, she can also enter more easily into the feelings of Mary at such a time. Far from kneeling collectedly at the manger, she would seem to be stretched flat out, in a state of mind and body in which exhaustion and invigoration, physical and emotional, are in total unison. Even if the theologians would traditionally have Jesus flip out somehow bypassing the hymen (and thus preserving Mary's virginity in an over-literal sense), they will surely allow her labour pains? Every woman feels she has done the cleverest thing in the world when she has produced a baby. Mary must have felt this too, especially if, as tradition imagines it, she had given birth in the difficult surroundings of a stable far from home, and if, further, she had foreknowledge of Jesus' importance and divine parentage. No angels filling the skies with Glorias could have equalled the singing in her heart. No new star moving over Bethlehem could have meant more than the invisible Spirit she felt shining down on this tiny spot in the universe.

Every mother knows reverence at the creation of her new-born baby, who is so obviously a person from the first moment she sees him. More reverence still would a mother feel if she could already see with the eyes of God all that her little child would grow to — the talent and beauty and strength and love that are already written into his make-up. When we contemplate the new-born Jesus we can find all that reverence and more. This child is a hope that comes to total fulfilment, a genetic potential that unfolds into the most admirable person the world has ever known; he is a promise that saves us from everything that will ever threaten us, and a prince who is to be raised to the right hand of God. We know that from this moment God is indeed with us.

Part Two

14

Prayer in the home

The first part of this book has been concerned with the experience of motherhood, told largely through my own story. It has been concerned with re-living that experience in all its vividness in order to look there the more deeply for pathways to God. It has been concerned with the mother's life, looked at from the standpoint of faith.

Now, in Part Two, I want to shift my gaze to the life of faith, looked at from the standpoint of a mother. I want to look at the practical means a mother can use to nourish and foster her spiritual life. I want to consider not just the God that can be found through motherhood, but the ways in which, as mothers, we can go about seeking her.

We all try to find the right way of being a Christian within our own life-calling, the right balance, for example, of reading, work, prayer and church-going. These are everyone's problems, but for mothers it is particularly hard to find a path. So few of our major Christian exemplars in history have been mothers, and within my own, Catholic tradition so few are even today. There are also the problems of time and place that constitute a more complex obstacle course than any celibate adviser could dream possible. For the mother, it has to be a matter of personal experiment in a largely uncharted ground, and it is easy to lose heart and lose interest. And yet I believe the mother has special gifts and special privileges for her spiritual life that more than outweigh her practical difficulties.

The three chapters of this second part will take three major ways in which we can feed our knowledge of God — by prayer, by sacrament, and by theology. I find it hard to imagine being a Christian without all three playing a part, and I describe the particular ways in which they have been important to me. But for others, particularly non-Catholic Christians, the balance might be different and other elements might come to the fore. What I speak of in this section is not meant to be normative for a mother's spirituality, but rather to reflect the ways in which I, in my own life, have been able to deepen my response to God. I share what I have found, and I speak from where I am now, but there is more to be found and my spiritual life is only one part of a wide range of possibilities. With the help of God and the inspiration of the Church, each one must find her own path.

*

The last chapter of the first part spoke of finding God in our homes. But we will not find God in our homes unless we stop and pray there. Prayer is probably the area of greatest difficulty in a lay person's spiritual life, and yet it is the prerequisite for a spiritual life at all. There must be few serious lay Christians who have not made an attempt at forming a place for prayer within their lives, but fewer still who have succeeded. We try, we wonder if anything is happening, we become discouraged, life takes over and we forget about it. All Christians would agree it was a good thing to pray, and yet there seem so few lay people who have found out how and when and where to do so. To pray — in the sense of stopping doing everything else in order to try to pray — seems, for a lay person, faintly eccentric. In those odd moments when we have furtively had a little go at it we have felt dry and useless, and so we soon opt for being normal and put out the milk bottles instead.

This chapter is not just another abstract exhortation to pray, but it is about praying in the home, praying as a lay person, praying as a mother. Most of it is simply about what I have found helped me. Some of what helped me may help others. Some of it may not. I offer it not as a programme, but as an experience. And yet I am sure that those who feel drawn to follow a similar path will find there what they seek.

There are two sub-sections within this chapter. The first deals with home retreats — the privileged and intense periods in my prayer life, which have laid down the foundations for all the rest. The second deals with the problem of

finding a place within the home where we can pray satis-
factorily: without some kind of sacred space the attempt to
form a regular habit of prayer can become an unnecessarily
uphill struggle. Without retreats I would not have begun to
pray; without a prayer place I would not have continued.

Retreats without going away

When I was having a hard and demanding time with the
children after Cordelia's birth, I found I had only one hour
to myself each day, between 6.30 and 7.30 in the evening,
when I had got the children to bed and did not yet have to
start making the supper. I did not want that hour to drift
away as it might have done if I had just used it to relax in; I
wanted to use it in the most actively personal way possible.
I decided to use it for prayer. If I had used it for something
creative like writing or sewing I would have found it frus-
tratingly short. But for prayer an hour is really quite a long
time. What is more I knew it was something I needed to
turn to sooner or later. I had not prayed for years. I had lost
any ability to pray. It was a little nag at the back of my conscience which I would be able to satisfy by working
seriously and regularly at prayer in my daily hour.

I read enough of the classical literature on the subject to
be encaptured by the determination to break in on this
world that was spoken of as so marvellous. For the first few
weeks I tried on my own with just the help of books and felt
I was getting nowhere. I knew I needed support and
teaching. I looked around for a teacher, I discussed the
matter with everyone I could think of — my confessor, and
other Dominicans at our church; a Benedictine who was
into mantras; an Orthodox priest who had written on
prayer, when he came to visit some friends . . . . Then Peter,
who had been a Jesuit, told me about the Spiritual Exercises
of St Ignatius.

In the full form of the Exercises you spend thirty days in
intensive retreat, talking over the fruits of your prayer with
a retreat-giver, and meditating on the matter he appoints
for you. This was clearly impossible for me, as I could not
leave the children, but the Exercises can also be done in
daily life, over a longer period of time. It was a big commit-

ment, but I did not mind about that. I wanted to do something big, so that I could look back at the end and see some progress.

I made three attempts to find someone to give me the Exercises from the local Jesuit house, but all without success. I rang up a Jesuit friend in London who worked in the field of spirituality. 'I want to do the Spiritual Exercises', I said, 'and no one will take me on.' He said 'Of course you must do the Spiritual Exercises if you want to', and he gave me lots of encouraging advice, none of which actually landed me with a retreat-giver, but it gave me the reassurance I needed. In the end Peter gave me the Exercises himself. We resisted this until it became inevitable, thinking there was something not quite right about being directed by your own husband, although we were not quite sure what. In fact it worked out very well: I was very happy with Peter's direction, and he kept it on a very detached level. Usually I would just leave my retreat journal lying about and he would skim over it and give me some brief notes on what to do next. It was good to be able to share something so important and intimate, even in this rather formal way. Perhaps most of all it was valuable to have daily direction. If I had had to go out to see a retreat-giver that would have robbed me of my prayer time for that day.

This first experience of the Exercises was characterized by nothing but dryness. I struggled through my daily hour, often falling asleep at my prayers, often disturbed by the children although they were meant to be in bed, often counting down the minutes until I would have finished my time. As directed, I wrote a short account of each meditation in a notebook and I seemed to write as often of my difficulties and disturbances in prayer as of any actual insight or glimmer of religious feeling. The retreat took four months from start to finish. Many other people engaged in doing the Exercises at home (under Annotation 19, as it is called) take a lot longer.

A '19th Annotation' retreat is much less intense than a closed retreat: you swing less rapidly and dramatically from highs to lows — from consolation to desolation, to use Ignatian terms. That makes it less of an 'experience', but it also brings fewer doubts and scruples about whether what is going on is genuine or not. The fruits of prayer are continually fed into and nourished by ordinary life. There is still a problem of absorption but it is not so acute. The events of the day can throw up material which enriches the evening's prayer. This interaction of prayer and living is encouraged.

There are many examples of the way life and prayer interacted in my retreat. One evening I was doing my meditation as I was babysitting in the house of some friends, sensing their vibes through all the objects of their house, so that I felt how much better I knew them now I had sat silently in their home without them even being there. I thought of how God's creation was like their creation of their house: we can sense God's vibes through the beauty of the world she has made, and so created things, far from being a distraction, can be a means to our knowledge and love of God. The seeming disturbance of having to go out and babysit while I was in retreat was in this way able to be turned to use.

I was able again to use an image from my everyday life as a mother when I was praying over the need to turn away from sin towards God. Cordelia was just at the stage of learning to crawl: she kept falling over, often hurting herself so that she cried, yet she could not give up, she never tired or became discouraged. That seemed to me a good image of what the Christian life should be: we should not become discouraged by our failures or by the unobservable rate of our progress. We will learn, as she learned to crawl, if we have a comparable inner compulsion, even if we cannot observe our improvement at the time.

I found the analogy of marriage helpful, as I prayed over the calling of the disciples. When you first become involved with someone you are drawn largely by fascination: you want to explore the relationship and see where it will lead. So the disciples went after Christ with a certain curiosity at first, not knowing what it would involve and with no chance to make a considered decision. So too we become Christians in our childhood: we are members of the Church before we have ever had a chance to think it through and decide for ourselves. But there comes a point in a relationship when you feel you have to make a choice: either you decide you have probed the relationship deeply enough and want to move on, or you commit yourself to probing it to its depths, making the ultimate, life-long commitment that alone can permit you to do that. Christian commitment is the same: in the end you have to decide that being a disciple of Christ means giving all your life to him, without keeping open the possibility of withdrawing from the commitment if things do not work out as you thought. Fascination, curiosity, attraction . . . they are essential at the beginning; but they are not the same as commitment.

As the retreat continued through the ministry and into the passion of Christ I found my own particular, maternal form of penance. The children both caught whooping cough, and I had to devote myself to constant nursing. We had to stay at home, because of the danger of infection, and I was naturally worried about their health, as well as feeling frustrated and reduced by the demands of their illness. Evening after evening my prayer was interrupted. One day I was called up to attend to them three times within the first twenty-five minutes of my attempted prayer. I found praying quite difficult enough anyway without this constant stopping and starting and anxiety over how long I would have until the next interruption. Eventually I had to suspend the Exercises altogether until the children began to recover, and when, a fortnight later, I picked up again in the middle of the Passion, I felt extraordinary reluctance and heavy-heartedness. I did not realize at the time how these external difficulties were being used for God's own purposes. It was no coincidence that these problems arose at just the point of the Exercises where penance is suitable, nor that the day on which I was at last able to return to the retreat was Ash Wednesday.

When I came to meditate on the resurrection and ascension I became even more discouraged. Naturally one thinks meditating on the resurrection should make one happy, but it can have the opposite effect. At Easter I always feel extremely happy, but then there is so much to affect my mood in terms of music and flowers and candlelight. An individual retreat, without even the company of a group in a retreat house, makes these meditations far more difficult, but it also gives a greater assurance of the genuineness of what is going on. I might be manipulated into feeling the joy of the resurrection at Easter, but here on my own, with nothing between me and the texts and God, I began to find out what I really felt about Jesus rising from the dead.

The retreat ends with a contemplation to lead us towards the love of God. Ignatius himself uses the analogy of a lover sharing all his worldly goods with his beloved. There was clearly a lot here that could be helped by my experience of loving Peter and the children. I observed how compulsively I needed to give to those I loved, and they to me, and when I thought about all that Peter had done for me, I loved him the more for it. I also observed how the more I loved my family, the more I was aware of the inadequacy of my love. So it is in our relationship with God. As we learn to recognize God's love for us we are moved to love her in return, and the more we love her the less adequate our love seems. Love grows the more it is exchanged.

By the time I had finished the retreat, I still could not see much evidence of the progress I had hoped for. I still felt prayer did nothing for me, and that I had not broken into its mystery. But over the course of the next months I began to notice an extraordinary change. Religion began to affect me, slowly and inescapably, in a way that had never happened before. I began to be deeply disturbed by the passion of Christ. I began to realize the awful commitment we make when we accept the cup of the covenant to drink. On the last page of my retreat journal I had written 'Perhaps I love Jesus'. It took a little over a year for me to realize unmistakably that I did. Dry and difficult as the Exercises had been at the time I did them, I gradually came to experience their power as they worked out their effect in me. Soon I came to realize that everything that deeply moved me about the Christian faith had taken its beginning from those barren hours of trying to pray and not knowing if I was succeeding: my faith had moved from my head to my heart.

I also realized that the Exercises were helping me to synthesize my life as a Christian with my life as a wife and mother. Ever since my schoolgirl conversion I had been looking for Christian beacons along the lay path, and had found very few of them. Now the Exercises were enabling me to find something for myself that no one could have handed on. In an Ignatian retreat you do not listen to addresses by someone else: you go into the desert on your own, while your retreat-giver sits in a nearby oasis to which you regularly return to refill your water bottle. What God wants from me, what God is saying to me, what Christianity means for me . . . are the questions you are battling out, and no one else can do it for you. And so it no longer mattered that there was not a prepared tradition of married and maternal spirituality that I found adequate. I had to find my own, and the Exercises helped me to do it.

Two years later, in Rome, I repeated the Exercises. Again I made them at home under Annotation 19, but this time in a more intense form that was more like a closed retreat. I could put aside three hours a day for prayer (weekends apart), but I soon found that praying for three hours each day meant you never really stopped praying at all. The retreat took me a month, but I felt so knocked about by the end that it was weeks before I could pick up the strands of my ordinary life again. Whereas my first retreat had been characterized by dryness, this one was filled with pain, but by the end I was very happy, if in a rather stunned way.

I was fortunate to have giving me the Exercises an Indian Jesuit who was something of a spiritual master. While I was wondering whether I dared ask such a busy and important man to take me on, my selfsame English Jesuit friend, who had encouraged me the first time, came to stay the night with us in Rome, and he said 'So what? You are a very busy woman. If you do not think you are worth his time that is your problem not his.' So of course I asked him and of course he said yes. I was to see him about every two or three days.

Again I found an astonishing interaction between my life and my prayer, even though the effect of the retreat was to make me withdraw — internally if not externally — from all that was around me for quite a long time. I began the retreat by finding myself full of anxieties about my family. They all seemed so vulnerable. What would I do if they died? I felt very weak, and in my act of commitment I could only passively put my hand into God's, recalling the simple trust with which my children do this, not knowing what will come.

As the retreat progressed I was astonished at the way the events of my daily existence held messages for me. Perhaps I might have chosen — if I had had the choice — to go away where there would be no letters or phone calls or engagements, but those that came turned out to be deeply important in complementing the experiences of my prayer life.

Of notable importance was the death of a friend's baby; the news acted as a reminder of my own worst fears. Over the next two days I prayed with desperate intensity. In ordinary life one can push these fears away and say 'It is so unlikely to happen to me', but in this retreat I had to stare death in the face in a way I had never done before — death of children, death of loved ones. It sounds incredible to say that, in the course of two or three days' prayer, fears as deep as this can be resolved, but perhaps this is something of what Jesus meant when he said prayer could move mountains. Little wonder that I wrote in my diary twenty-four hours later 'So much, so much happening, I can't believe the pace', and that twenty-four hours after that I was so exhausted that I could only lay myself down as a tiny baby, seeking rest and sleep on the warm breast of my mother.

Even when I had to go out I found that God could use these exits to the advantage of the retreat. Praying in the chapel of the Gregorian University (where I had gone for a class) I was affected by the golden spikes radiating out of the tabernacle, calling me in past them to the heart where the body of Christ lay broken in death; praying in the Basilica of SS. Cosmas and Damian (where I had gone for a commemoration mass of Archbishop Romero's death) I was moved by the great sixth-century Christ in the apse above the altar, stretching out his hand and simultaneously inviting me and judging me, encouraging me and restraining me, guiding me and blessing me. Even bowling along the polluted streets of Rome on my motorbike God found a way of speaking to me, as my bike went into a massive pothole and threw me off into the stream of traffic. You do not have to be in the beautiful isolation of a country retreat house to be alone with God: it can happen in a busy city street.

As for the children, they sometimes helped, and even

when they hindered it was striking how little it mattered. One night when I had been praying away for days, feeling nothing, understanding nothing and worrying about how long I must wait before I would understand what God was up to, I looked out of the children's room at the sunset and thought that if God had written 'Repent' or 'Rejoice' in the sky it could not be clearer. Cordelia came in and straight away chortled with glee and pointed out of the window. I could not believe that she was responding to quite an everyday sunset when she had never paid the slightest attention to such things before, but at last she said 'The sky — I like it — the sky'. Five minutes later when the pink had turned to the dull dark grey of evening Cordelia again turned to the window, again completely unprompted, and said 'Oh, sky gone away'. I said 'Will it come back?' She said 'Yes'. I said 'When?' She said 'Soon. Soon. Jesus will make it come back.' So in my state of impatience and puzzlement God spoke to me through Cordelia. God would come again, soon.

When a few days later, God did come again, and I was swept up into the richness of Christ's appearance to Mary Magdalen, not even constant interruptions from the children could halt the flow of my responses. As I wrote about that appearance in my journal I made a note every time that the children made me stop in what I was writing — sometimes making me stop until the next day — but the words rush on as though there is no interruption at all.

We do not need the protection of a retreat house to become totally involved in the excitement of God's word. Doing a retreat at home is more difficult, and of course we wish we were not interrupted, but in God's great providence it may provide the very circumstances that God wishes to use to speak to us. Going into retreat is not a geographical move, it is an interior decision. If we seek God, and give time to that search, and use the help of the Church in the form of a retreat-giver — so that we have the reassurance that we are not just embarking on a self-directed ego-trip — then God will speak to us. Sometimes she speaks loudly so that we are overwhelmed, and sometimes, for whatever reason, we cannot hear her speak at all, but in time we will hear her, and then we will know that for us, in our situation, in our calling in life, in our stage of development, there is no better way that she could have spoken to us.

Perhaps we feel drawn to making a retreat but fear that heights of prayer and long hours of meditation are not for us. I am not sure that they are for me either, but we do not all need to launch straight out into the full Spiritual Exercises, for there is endless flexibility in ways of adapting them and abridging them, so that there is a version of Ignatian retreat suitable for the needs of all. But for that we will need to find a good retreat-giver to direct us, and that may not be easy. (Reading the book of the Exercises is worse than useless — it can be very harmful without guidance.) The nearest Jesuit house is the best place to start looking.

But whether we choose a long retreat or a short one, a '19th Annotation' retreat or a closed one, the Ignatian approach is very suitable for our needs as lay people. First, there is the stress on finding our own personal and individual way of relating to God, so that we do not feel we have to fit a hole before we start; it is not a spirituality for groups or for movements but for private individuals. Then there is the principle of finding God in all things, in all the experiences of our daily life; living 'in the world' becomes the setting for finding God — a pathway to her, strewn with tokens of her love. Then there is the recognition that contemplation is not only for professionals; an occasional period of more intense prayer — which is what a retreat is — can bring the most ordinary of us to a short-term comtemplative experience, and leave us strengthened and confirmed in our life in the home, as lay people and mothers. After that, in our ordinary daily routine, we will not need long hours of disciplined prayer, but a few minutes of quiet recollection, in a place where we can feel at home with God.

Prayer places

We may find God in our home simply by being still and praying there. Perhaps we have come down in the middle of the night for a glass of water, and we just sit at the kitchen table for a while, sensing the presence of the sleeping family above us, seeing the signs of their daily living around us in the room, and feeling the heartbeat of the house all the more strongly for the fact that it is at rest. Sometimes then we can be aware that there is something more than people and objects here — an indwelling, a glow of care and blessedness that hovers around this centre of family life and sanctifies it. Or perhaps we have found a regular spot within the house where we pray deliberately and systematically: a cushion on the floor, an upright chair by a table, a mat at the foot of the bed. Then we need to feel assured that God can inhabit this spot just as surely as she can dwell in the church or on the mountain; we need to find a way of moving from the vibrations of bustling activity to the still presence of God who lies at the heart of them.

It is not easy to make this move, however legitimate it is. Many people, and I am one of them, find it much easier to pray by going into a chapel and entering straight away into the quiet stillness that someone else has left behind and that has hung like incense, undisturbed by other activity. In the days when some people had big, grand houses they would be able to build a chapel within their house, but few people can afford today to set aside a whole room as a chapel. Nevertheless it may be worthwhile to look for some corner of the house that could be set aside for prayer, and where you could be undisturbed even if other people are moving around the house.

One family we know, who were fortunate enough to have a large house, had a little attic room where no one ever went unless there were visiting school friends, sleeping on mattresses. One Sunday when a priest was staying we all went up there and had a eucharist together, in great quiet and peace. The attic had sloping white eaves and beams and bare boards on the floor, and a tiny window at the end through which you could only look by crouching down on the floor. I do not know if they ever used it privately for prayer but it would have been an ideal place, perched between the earth of their home life and the heaven of the skies, a part of the house and yet a secret part, a place of withdrawal which yet remained under the security of the family roof.

The first home prayer place I came across — exclusively

set aside as such — was in a converted pig-sty at my god-mother's home. Although her house is not small she has as many as ten members of the family living there in holidays, so there is not room to turn over a room in the house just for prayer. In fact it was one of her daughters who decided to make this little prayer hut in the garden. To get in you must go on hands and knees through a door designed for pigs, and inside are a few little stools and a low wooden chair. There is a shelf for bibles and prayer books and candles and a lighter that does not work. Then there is a window with honeysuckle growing through it and a crucifix hanging below. One wall is a partition dividing it from the wood-shed, and the struts on it form a big cross. The ceiling starts low and ends high, like an arrow pointing towards heaven. You must share your place of prayer with a fair number of earwigs and spiders, but strangely I minded that much less than I would have thought, and undeniably in the air hovers the presence of God. Prayer leaves a very special atmos-phere behind.

When I came home from Italy I made my own prayer place in our house. I had thought about it for a long time, ever since I visited the pig-sty prayer hut some eighteen months before, and I finally set it up during one Holy Week. It is in an under-the-stairs cupboard, right at the bottom of the house, in the basement, half below ground level, but with a grating to the outside air. I had already got the builders to damp-proof it, whitewash it, put in a light and extend the carpeting. Now to turn it into a place of prayer I put there a candle and a crucifix and I stuck some religious postcards on the wall. The crucifix was carved by a friend and given to Peter years before, and the postcards each have a special meaning for me. There is a Fra Angelico painting of a friar with his fingers to his lips, saying 'Shh . . .' as you go in the door — crouching, for the cupboard is only four feet high. There is an anchor and a dove from the cata-combs — those early, underground sacred places that meant so much to me when I visited them in Rome. There is a Madonna and child, also from the catacombs — the earliest painting of Mary in the world. There is the face on the Shroud, which I believe may be truly that of Jesus, and which shows me a man more impressive than any in

Christian art. There is a picture of each of our saints: Peter, crucified upside down, from a diptych by Giotto; Paul, beheaded, from the same diptych, and representing Dominic's second name; Dominic himself, by Fra Angelico, chosen by my own Dominic as his favourite out of all his vast collection of paintings of his saint; Anna, for Anna Cordelia, in a detail from the beautiful Holy Family by Leonardo; Benedict, a reproduction of uncertain origin on a loose page from a book of saints handed on to me by my godmother years ago after her own children had finished with it; only Margaret herself is so far lacking, but since Mary is my third name I have some representation. Then there is a little design of coloured shapes stuck on paper that Cordelia made 'for Jesus'. Overhead, hanging over a pipe, is the branch that was blessed at this year's Palm Sunday. On the floor are three or four cushions for sitting on, and a little pile of missals, bibles and the like. A curtain separates off the part of the cupboard that I still need as a storage place, and a changing sequence of vases of flowers symbolizes every sort of prayer that I would like to make and cannot. They stay in the presence of God after I have gone, and they are there when I return.

When I sit in this little, low prayer place, facing the crucifix and the Shroud face, with the lighted candle below them and a narrow shaft of light from the grating slanting down from above, then I feel a great sense of spaciousness. Around may be the noises of the house — the children running in and out of the garden and sending shadows over the grating as they do so ... the washing machine, humming and glugging through the floor a few feet above my right shoulder ... the neighbours, who for some reason can be heard more clearly here than through any other section of the party wall. But I feel I am resting here in the centre of things, in the hidden centre of my home, in the secret centre of my soul, and that centre is a place of calm and light and space. Sometimes I stay less than a minute, sometimes more than half an hour. I am called away from it as often as I leave voluntarily. But I like to know it is there, even when I am not in it. Just to think of the place for a moment is a prayer.

I need my prayer hole because I am bad at praying. (When

I was in Rome one of my lecturers said 'You think you're no good at prayer? I'll tell you a secret — I've been around a long time — there ain't nobody who's any good at prayer. Prayer is a mystery.') I need it because I can just go in and do nothing and then I am praying. It takes the effort out of it, and the dread, and the fear of boredom, and the distractions. It cuts down the interruptions too: when I am in my prayer hole people do not burst in on me. If they need me they call respectfully. They do not break in on that fragile vulnerable core of being that we need to let unfold gently in the sight of God. Of course this can be done without a special place, but I find it easier with one, and that, for me, is quite sufficient reason for a somewhat uncommon — but possibly a growing — practice.

15

Sacraments

Private prayer is not enough on its own, and we cannot be Christians on our own: we need also to pray together as a community and as a church. The sacraments are the most privileged moments of this community prayer, because there events of human significance are taken up into the life of the Church and, through the Church, taken up into the life of God. That makes it all sound very abstract, but the point of the sacraments is that they are very concrete: you see something, you hear something, you feel something, and through these material actions a profound spiritual change is taking place.

In this chapter I speak from my experience of three sacraments — baptism, the eucharist and reconciliation. Baptism has enabled me to bring my children into the Church that means so much to me, while the eucharist and reconciliation regularly feed my own spiritual life with the riches that can only come from the community. As always, I speak as a mother, dwelling on the particular role each sacrament can play in a mother's life, with both the problems and the privileges that life brings. The precious moments of love and sharing as a mother are rediscovered in the sacraments — rediscovered, sanctified and shared more widely — so that what we do in the sacraments is the perfecting of what we do in the heart of our family.

Baptizing our babies

Catholics are notorious for being anxious about getting their babies baptized. There has been so much theological discussion about what happens to unbaptized babies if they die. Do they go to hell because there is no salvation outside baptism? Or to heaven because they are innocent and have not sinned? Or to some compromise place called Limbo, because they cannot go to either heaven or hell?

All Catholics are taught how to do an emergency baptism if there is no priest around, and how the water must flow. It can be tea or beer if you like, but it must flow. I remember hearing a sermon in my youth about a doctor who had thought he had baptized dozens of tiny babies, and liked to think of them all in heaven, praying for the man who saved them. But unfortunately he thought all you had to do when you said the words was to make the sign of the cross over them. And so, the sermon finished chillingly, 'he had not baptized any of them'.

It can sound absurd when talked about like that, but I must admit I was extremely relieved to get my babies baptized, and they were all done at about four weeks of age. Pope John XXIII was baptized on the day he was born, which I suppose reflects an extreme of importance attached to the act of baptism itself, irrespective of who can come to share in the event. When I was a child a fortnight was considered the right age. Considering the mother is not properly up and about until about two weeks after the birth, a baptism that is to involve the mother can hardly be done earlier. At my own baptism — at a fortnight — there were present only parents and godparents, my brother, my grandmother and the priest. That is a very beautiful, intimate way to do a baptism, but Peter and I felt that with the insights coming out of post-conciliar thinking the community should be present to welcome the new member into the Church. Organizing a party can hardly be done earlier than a month after the birth, so it is evident that we were falling into the typical Catholic pattern of getting our children baptized at the first possible moment. It is not that I believe in Limbo, but that I feel all is not quite well until the child has joined the family of God. Seeing the baptized baby as a little innocent, whose cleansed soul will rise straight to heaven if it dies, is for me a touching picture of something deeper that I cannot put into words. I wanted my children baptized, I wanted it positively, and I do think in some way that cannot be pinned down they are different because of it.

Dominic and Cordelia were both immersed, not quite totally, but as much of them as would fit into the bowl that was used as a font. There is a strong symbolism in completely stripping off and going right into the water naked. In the early Christian Church even adults would be baptized that way, in the darkness of the night before the dawn of Easter; then when they emerged from the waters of the baptistery they were dressed in a white robe to symbolize the newness of life with Christ. The clothing in a white garment is kept in the modern liturgy, but it is usually done by putting a white shawl over the christening robe; I insisted at all our baptisms that the symbolism of the garment should concur with the symbolism of local custom, and it was the beautiful embroidered christening robe that had been worn for three generations that was the new robe put on the child.

The baptisms, like our wedding, were liturgies that we could organize for ourselves, and it was satisfying to be able to put something of ourselves into the way they were celebrated. At the baptism of Dominic, Peter and I each spoke a few words at the beginning of the mass about how we understood baptism. We chose all our own readings and music, and even had a sung eucharistic prayer that our priest — a specialist liturgist and gifted musician — had learned from the Dutch. For Cordelia's baptism Peter wrote a special piece of music to words that I had put together from the gospels and from *King Lear*. 'Fairest Cordelia, that art most rich being poor, most choice forsaken, and most loved despised' was the refrain, interspersed with the beatitudes: 'Blessed are the poor in spirit, for theirs is the kingdom of heaven . . . . Blessed are those who mourn, for they shall be comforted . . .'.

Our third baby, Benedict, was baptized only six weeks ago as I write. What reading time I had in the fortnight after his birth went into learning about the early baptismal rite and studying fourth-century baptismal sermons, in a book by Edward Yarnold SJ, *The Awe-inspiring Rites of Initiation* (St Paul Publications, Slough, 1972). That was when baptism really meant something, and I had a much stronger sense the third time round of the inadequacy of my preparation for this event in which I was to take vows on behalf of my child. However, one has to make the best of the available circumstances, and the time after the birth of a child is not exactly a moment when one can rush off into retreat. One just has to find a way in which the physical, time-consuming caring for a baby, and the natural anxieties and upheaval of the early weeks, can be a token of the spiritual preparation we would make if we were all disembodied spirits.

Benedict was born exactly four weeks before Easter, so we had him baptized at the Easter Vigil. It was beautiful and powerful, and I hope when he is older it will mean as much to him as it does to me to know that at this annual renewal of baptismal vows we celebrate the actual anniversary of his first vows, and that at this reliving of the mystery of our resurrection in Christ he first entered into the new life of the Church. And yet for this wonderful religious moment there were endless worries and plans and changes of plans. Would he cry all the way through the Vigil and spoil it for everyone else? Could Dominic and Cordelia come and see their little brother baptized? Would the relatives and friends who could not come at such an inconvenient time be offended? Would the worries of managing the baby detract from the concentration I would like to give to the most moving liturgy in the whole year? How would we get round the problem of the white garment, when we could not make everyone wait for ages while we did up lots of little buttons and pulled up lots of little drawstrings? How and when and where and with whom would we do the preliminary anointing and giving of the name that would have to be done before the Vigil itself? What would I wipe Benedict's nose with if it was running when I picked him up? There are times when I wish we *were* disembodied spirits.

I expect I fuss too much, but it was only by planning a way through all these tedious problems that the whole event was as successful and beautiful as it was. We put Dominic and Cordelia to bed on mattresses at the church, with my mother left to watch over them. 'When we wake you up', I said, 'it will be the middle of the night, and Jesus will have risen from the dead. Benedict was born in the night, now he is going to be born again in the night. I will come and bring you into the church, and it will be full of people and flowers, and you will sit with Grandma and Grandpa right at the front and see Benedict baptized.'

Benedict cried for a couple of hours in the early evening, but by the time we went to the Vigil he was in a deep sleep. Not even when I lifted him up and carried him out in front of the altar did he wake, but when the water trickled over his forehead he opened his eyes and looked up at me with a great peace. I like to remember that moment, surrounded by light and happiness in the depths of the night, when the hundreds of Christians that packed our church took a few minutes at the most sacred moment of the year to pray over and bless and welcome my little baby, and to call down on him the wholeness of the salvation won by Christ's resurrection from the dead.

The eucharist

Those of us who have grown up in a sacramental tradition have come to rely very strongly on the eucharist as a privileged moment for meeting God. In motherhood this need of the eucharist can be felt particularly acutely, not only because the mother has so many intense experiences to bring into the healing calm of God's presence, but also because it becomes increasingly difficult for a mother to get to church and receive the sacrament. At the very period when a mother has most need of spiritual and sacramental support, she can feel most starved of it.

It is perhaps ironic that the Churches that offer the eucharist tend to be those with the least sensitivity to the practical needs of the mother. The more evangelical denominations are often the ones that provide crèches during services, and the Quakers would not dream of holding a meeting without making provision for children. Meanwhile Catholic mothers have to face the dilemma of bringing their noisy children to mass and feeling embarrassed and distracted at the disturbance they may cause, or of finding someone else to look after them week after week after week. It is tragic but hardly surprising if they decide it is all too difficult and complicated and do not go at all.

In our Dominican church in Oxford we are fortunate enough to have a family mass, to which anyone can bring as many awful children as they want. Sometimes the children rush around climbing over choir stalls and eating unconsecrated hosts, but the idea is that no one should mind. One may be distracted, very distracted in fact, but at least one will not be embarrassed. Moreover the mass is organized in a way that is more appealing to children: the altar is half way down the church, with chairs on three sides; it is covered in a brightly patterned cloth with a large selection of colourful candles; little girls in pigtails trip around in over-long surplices as altar servers; and all the little children go out to draw pictures during the sermon. It is a tremendous help to have such a mass regularly available, and it has proved extremely popular over a period of many years, not only for families but also for many others without children who appreciate the tolerant atmosphere. But it does not solve every problem. Sometimes my children have refused to go out without me which has meant I have had to miss the sermon and listen to kiddie talk instead — usually now Peter takes them out and manages to slip back, but children go through different phases and it has not always been like that. And often I have longed for the quiet, more meditative atmosphere of the evening community mass, and been quite unable to leave the children at such a time. The Sunday morning romp is very lively and imaginative, but being with small children all day makes one look forward to something more adult for one's encounters with God.

Although the mother has such problems in getting to mass she brings with her an experience of life that gives richness and perspective to the eucharistic mysteries. The eucharist is a very physical event, concerned with the body and with blood and with eating. These things make up the stuff of a mother's life. She is in intimate relationship with bodies whether making love, or giving birth, or cleaning bottoms, or wiping noses. She is surrounded by physicality from the moment she wakes up to find hot little bodies squeezing into bed next to her, to the evening scramble of getting those dirty little wriggling bodies washed and dried and put into pyjamas and chased upstairs to bed. She has her share of blood too, as the children fall and cut themselves and then pick off their scabs. As for eating, literally hours of her life each day go in shopping and planning meals, cooking and serving up food, clearing the table and washing up the dishes. The elements of the eucharist lie at the centre of a mother's life, boringly central, even grindingly tediously central.

When in the eucharist we eat and drink of the body and blood of Christ, these central elements of our daily life are taken up and blessed and transformed. The hard work of daily child-minding is offered up with the bread and wine on the altar and given back to us in a new way. Our sense of harassment and frustration is soothed, and the threat of tedium is dissolved. Our petty troubles are dwarfed by the bloody sacrifice of Christ's body — a sacrifice that turned out to be not destructive but life-giving, not meaningless but healing. After such a transcendent meaning has been shown to us, and continuously re-lived in the regular celebration of the eucharist, bodies and blood, eating and drinking, will never be the same again.

The mother can also draw on her memories of breastfeeding to deepen her experience of the eucharist. She has known what it means to give of herself as food and drink, and has seen how totally absorbed her child is to receive the gift. She has seen how it has to stop crying to feed, and how even if it is in real pain it is willing to stop its howls and accept comfort if the breast is put in its mouth. Once it is feeding there is nothing else in the world that matters.

So, when we eat and drink of God herself we become totally absorbed in that act, and nothing else matters. We become quiet in the union with God, as our baby becomes quiet at our breast. We savour and relish and enjoy the food that strengthens and comforts us and that leads us into the greatest possible intimacy with our true mother. We leave aside our complaints, our pains and our worries, because we are aware of only one thing: the God, who is with us and within us, and who is our food and drink.

If, as mothers, we have our own experiences to bring to the understanding of the eucharist, we can make this link between our life and our religion in a very special way when mass is said in our homes. Among the early Christians there were no churches and the eucharist would always take place in a private house, and we are now re-discovering some of the values of bringing this holy moment into the heart of our everyday living. The sacred is not disguised by the setting of an ordinary room, but rather thrown into relief. No one wants to abolish churches, but the house mass can be a helpful supplement to the Sunday liturgy with the wider community.

As well as the attic mass I mentioned in the last chapter, I have been to masses in bedrooms, dining rooms, kitchens, sitting rooms and studies. When we have a priest to visit us in our own house we sometimes ask him to say mass for us, and then we usually sit around the kitchen table, and use a little bit of our ordinary bread and the wine that we will drink at dinner. Sometimes we have had children's masses in our home, but I like it best when we have put them to bed and can gather ourselves quietly in the presence of God before sharing a meal.

What means most to me about these occasions is the finding of God among the ordinary objects of my life. Of course I know that God is here with me always and that I can remember her presence in prayer at any moment, but never do I have a stronger sense of this than when the body of Christ is lying there on one of my own plates on my own kitchen table. It is difficult to be false at a house mass, or to keep God in a special compartment away from the rest of our lives. It is difficult too to stand at a distance from the events, as a spectator. We face each other across the table, we pass around the bible or missal to share the readings and share our thoughts on them afterwards, we each bring our own concerns before God as we make a contribution to the prayers. God speaks to all of us individually, and we all have some contribution to make to the building up of the body of Christ. As mothers, we must listen to God in the experience of our own motherhood; then perhaps we will be able to share something with the community that no one else can bring.

Reconciliation

Every mother knows a great deal about her inadequacies. Every day she is faced with her failures towards her children — I have already spoken a great deal about this in earlier chapters. She knows that she cannot even get everything right with those she most loves and cares for, let alone with those more distant from her whom she could hurt without even noticing. She knows a lot about failure in a close adult relationship too, with the father of her children — whether that relationship has ended up happy and permanent, or has broken up. She is likely to notice her failures most when they occur in these close relationships, with those whom she least wants to let down.

Just as the mother knows a lot about hurting and being hurt she also knows a lot about reconciliation. She knows that when you love someone there is no way you can accept an alienation in the relationship. The strain of being angry with someone you love, whether it is your child or your husband, drives you in a very short time to seek reconciliation, even if it means abandoning the position you have just conscientiously staked out as not open to negotiation. If you can laugh and hug and say sorry, the points of difficulty find a way of sorting themselves out. First be reunited, then resolve the differences: it is not always as simple as that, but it often is.

But whether that works or not as a technique for solving arguments, the point is that you seek reconciliation because you need to, because you cannot endure the expenditure of energy and the inner tension of not doing so. Anger burns you up but it passes. You need to take your children in your arms and kiss them before they go to bed. You need to give your husband a friendly pat before you can get to sleep. Reconciliation is not something mathematical, a willed decision to accept (a) if he or she will accept (b). It is a fountain of tenderness that breaks out again and again from within, cooling anger, softening bitterness, washing away what does not really belong to us and leaving a sense of peace behind. There comes a moment when it does not terribly matter what we have said or done or what we fear might happen between us in the future. What matters is that here and now we should be reconciled.

When you can seek and find perfect reconciliation between yourself and your family you do not, strictly speaking, need a sacrament for those particular hurts and faults. But human reconciliation is rarely perfect, and there is much sin that slips through the net of family love. Even within the family circle there is a lot to be sorry for that cannot be adequately expressed, especially when it comes to your children. You can embrace them and make them feel all right again after an argument, but you cannot give them a sense of how much you hope you are not damaging their personalities and exposing yourself to their future adolescent rejection. And certainly when it comes to the wider community we have no adequate way of apologizing for our failures. We can just about manage to say sorry to someone we know if we are aware of having failed the demands of friendship, but we cannot go out to the millions of starving people in the world and say how sorry we are that we did not give more to Oxfam. We cannot see all the damage we do, though we would like to say sorry for the sins we are unaware of as well as those that we can see and rectify. There is a vast gap between the reconciliation we would like to have with others, the world and God, and the little we can achieve given our physical and moral limitations. That is why we have a sacrament of reconciliation: it fills that gap.

The sacrament of reconciliation or penance or confession, as it is variously called, has been so badly exercised, so meaninglessly and trivially reduced to an expression of sins we hardly think are sins at all and an expression of contrition in high-flown language which we cannot possibly feel, that in practical terms of human experience it has rarely filled that gap. But slowly and somewhat clumsily the Catholic Church is beginning to find a more meaningful form for the sacrament. Confessions are happening less often but when they do they take longer and are less impersonal, often on an appointment system that brings them closer to spiritual direction. People are learning to bring more of their real selves into the confession they make, sometimes saying more to express the difficulties and ambiguities of a situation more adequately, sometimes allowing themselves to be driven into inarticulacy. Priests are learning to use more of their ordinary human capacities for compassion and understanding and support as well as drawing on the extraordinary gift of mediating divine mercy that has always managed to come through even the briefest of box confessions. The maturing of confessional practice is taking time, but there can be no doubt that it has begun.

When confession does find a meaningful sacramental expression, the experience of forgiveness can be quite astounding. I have sometimes woken in the night after going to confession, bowled over by the surprise of the forgiveness that I did not even know I wanted. When a friend or a husband forgives you you feel much better, but when God forgives you and the awareness of it hits you, mediated by one person whose compassion represents that of the whole Church and of God, then you just cannot believe that you have needed it so much. Sin is not that simple, you have thought; contrition is not that simple; reform is not that simple. But when reconciliation comes despite your incapacity to be simple about sin and sorrow, then problems and doubts do not seem that relevant any more. Yesterday they were relevant; they needed a place in the sacrament; they needed to be expressed. But once expressed they do not seem to matter much. All that matters is that God holds you in her loving embrace. First be re-united; then resolve the differences.

The experience of reconciliation within the home enriches the sacrament, and is enriched by it. The sacrament spreads the awareness of hurt and re-union outwards, towards all those people whom we may have offended but about whom we do not care so intensely as we do about our own family. It deepens and intensifies the experience of forgiveness as we know it belongs to the transcendent sphere, to God and her love, and not just to our family and their love. And yet in such spreading out and transcendent extending it is an intensely personal moment. It is our own sacrament, personally and privately and exclusively ours, when we are not swept up into a line of people whose dispositions we may or may not share, but when our difficulties, our doubts, our unworthinesses become not a barrier to relating to God, but the very matter of that deepening involvement. As lay women we can sometimes feel very alone in relating to God and the Church, and in confession that loneliness is taken up and understood and blessed. We belong more deeply to the Christian community for having been allowed something so personal and private; we feel more a part of the family of God for having taken the time and effort to put ourselves individually as a child before God in the presence of our Christian brother.

16

Theology

It is by prayer — private prayer and community prayer — that we communicate with God, but without any intellectual stimulation that communication will lack richness. A little theological input — how much depends on the inclination of each of us — can permit us to explore our relationship with God more confidently. To take the obvious example from the theme of this book — theology can allow us to think of God as our mother, and that thought can then lead us into a secure awareness of her protective care, and so help us feel closer to her.

I have studied theology more than most mothers would wish to. At times perhaps I have lost sight of the reason for studying it, and then, studying more, I have been reminded and brought back to my aim. This chapter recounts my own theological training, and then dwells on the one particular topic of God's mothering of us, showing how it is by no means my own invention but is deeply rooted in the tradition of the Church.

*

When I was twenty-one and already in my third year at Oxford University I gave up my previous degree course and began to study theology instead. There was a sense of home-coming about it, in that it was what I had always wanted to do and had not done only because it seemed too obvious. I was of course that way inclined even in my schoolgirl agnostic period: theological speculation has always involved me even aside from my own committed faith. But for a Christian who is intellectually inclined it is natural to want to bring together one's faith and one's mind, one's believing and one's thinking.

For three years I read theology and philosophy at Oxford: it was a rigorous academic training, in which one tried hard to keep one's intellectual purity by not letting anything slip out that might indicate that one actually believed in what one was talking about. I valued such an approach at the time, and it did mean that a lot of loose thinking was kept out of the way. You could not substitute piety for argument. It also meant that questions could be faced with a fearless honesty. You could not shock anyone in the theology faculty. Outsiders could be shocked, and indeed were, especially by the questioning of incarnation language that centred around the figure of Maurice Wiles, the Regius Professor of Divinity. But fearless honesty, I believed, could never damage true faith. Daring questions were a test of personal integrity. One day, in a tutorial with the Professor of Moral and Pastoral Theology, I mentioned the soul. He buried his head in his hands for a long time, and then said in a voice of troubled sincerity 'I am not sure I know what a soul is'.

After my degree, and by now married, I continued to work on my theology at home. Shortly after the birth of Dominic I was asked to co-author a short book on the sacrament of penance. It was the last topic I would have chosen, but it turned out to be a godsend. It opened my mind to the richness of Catholic theology (although I made the book as inter-denominational as possible). I began to realize the importance of the sacraments, and the naivety of the misunderstandings that made them a point of contention at the Reformation. I started to feel the strength of our spiritual dependence upon one another — Christian upon Christian. I began to unlock the riches of our earlier history, and realized that it is often what someone said fifteen centuries ago that can have more relevance to our current problems than the blinkered circularity of the modern discussion. I was led to re-examine my own life in a way I never would have done if I had not had to study this particular branch of theology: I could not write about confession without going to confession, and that meant looking again at various aspects of my life that I had thought I was too busy to do anything about at the moment. And so I was led to new topics that would involve me spiritually as well as theologically, and in particular the study of prayer, of which I have already spoken.

After that there was a brief lull. I thought I would have to sacrifice theology now I was so busy with two little children. In fact while my mind was frustrated I found I had less to give the children, and when we went to Rome a little after Cordelia's first birthday this seemed an unrepeatable opportunity to study theology in another country, in another style of university with a different approach.

The Gregorian University in Rome is run mostly by Jesuits but the students come from dioceses all over the world and from every sort of religious order. Much of its work is concerned with training priests, but there are also many sisters and some laity. I joined post-graduate classes in English, picking out what I thought would be valuable for me from a huge range of possibilities. Some of my lectures were classed as theology, some as spirituality, some as Christian art and some as ecclesiastical history. The academic standards — given the diversity of the background — were not of course as uniformly severe as they had been at Oxford, though they were far from low. The main difference from Oxford was the sense of common mission. We were all Catholics, but more than that we knew that we were all there because we loved God and wanted to serve the Church. Theology was the preparation for our ministry, whether that ministry was to teach in a seminary in the USA, to work for the Indians in the sweltering jungles of Brazil, or to come back to a family home in Oxford.

The moment I first became acutely aware of this was on the morning after the shooting of Archbishop Oscar Romero, who had been gunned down as he was saying mass in El Salvador. I had just been feeling profoundly alienated from the Greg because the Vatican had taken action against two important Catholic theologians, Hans Küng and Edward Schillebeeckx, and in all the university there had not been so much as a minority protest petition. (It later turned out that the Pope had signed the condemnation of Küng's theology on the very day he had come to visit the Greg and been clapped and cheered.) But, as we gathered in the great hall for a short prayer service for Romero, that sense of disillusion became relativized. We said the Lord's Prayer in Latin and then dispersed for our next lecture, and I felt from the very matter-of-fact way in which it was done that it could be any of us who were next. We were not all going out to countries where the Church was persecuted (though some of us were) but we were all bound together in one communion where death and even martyrdom were recognized as a reality of Christian life. Strengthened by each other, we accepted it.

The theology I have studied — both the rigorous, philosophical discipline of Oxford before I was a mother, and the more ministerially directed training in Rome when I already had two children — has gone to influence the way I think about God and the choice of things I say about her. Theology, as I understand it, is talk about God. Anything we say about God has theological suppositions and implications. When we study theology we pay more conscious attention to making our talk about God coherent and rich. We do this through many sub-disciplines — analysing the biblical literature . . . reading the works of our theological fore-fathers . . . articulating the theological implications of liturgy, religious art and music, mysticism . . . relating the things we want to say about God to things philosophers want to say about existence . . . .

Theology can reach a point at which it loses touch with the fertile ground of Christianity from which it springs, and instead it becomes barren and, very rapidly, boring. Much theology, even much modern theology, has gone this way. But we cannot do without theology, because we cannot do without talking about God. The opposite danger is to become engrossed in churchy matters, and that is a falsification too. The work of the Church is only interesting in so far as it is concerned with God and with preaching the gospel of Jesus Christ. Theology continually re-centres us on our subject-matter and helps us to absorb the problems of self-understanding that arise in our Christian work.

For me one of the chief problems of self-understanding has been to combine the knowledge of myself as lay person and mother, with the knowledge of myself as a Christian engaged upon studies that are usually more or less reserved to priests and sisters. I have had to learn to re-centre myself on God and my faith in a way that is true to my mind and at the same time true to my experience. This book represents the fruits of that attempt. Clearly I could never have written a book like this if I had not been through the experience of motherhood. But I am also sure that I could not have written it if I had not studied theology. I might have thought of calling God our mother, but I would have lacked the confidence to explore the idea systematically. I would also have lacked the imagination to do so, because while I concentrate on the particular theme of divine motherhood I am continually sparked off by what other people have said about God even while they have been exploring other themes.

Theology is a conversation, in which the ideas of one person inspire a response from another, agreeing and expanding, on the one hand, or making a reservation or a contrary suggestion on the other. As thinking beings we cannot live without conversation. It does not need to be lengthy talk; it needs rather to be good.

And so, when I call God mother, I am responding to what other people have said to me about her. Some people may have said things that make me want to restore the right balance by introducing a different idea. Other people have said things that make me want to take their ideas one stage further. But all the time I am learning the art of conversation from listening: I hear what others say, the way they develop feelings into thoughts and thoughts into words, the art of reasoning and the art of communicating. I find out whose conversational methods I would like to imitate, and whose I would like to reject.

Two important principles from the art of theological conversation have determined the methodology of this book. Firstly, theologians are aware that when we talk about God we use analogy. This means that we can use many different images or models for understanding God without worrying too much about how they all fit together. I can call God 'she' all the way through this book, and yet say 'he' when I next go to church, without any sense of discordance. I can call God 'mother' and yet pray the 'Our Father', without any sense of inconsistency. It is only an analogy. It is to help us. We cannot examine God and give a definitive judgement: 'He is really male'; 'She is really female'; 'It is really neuter'. God is all three of them, or none of them. But God is not nothing. God is God. God is.

The second principle is that theology should be based on experience. This is so often said in theological discussion today that it is rapidly becoming a truism. But the odd thing is, nobody seems to do it. The more theologians talk about experience, the less they seem to refer to it. I have read learned articles, translated from the German, all about theology and experience, and found them so stodgy that I could barely wade through them. And so, when I decided to write this book, I determined that if it claimed to be based on experience it should really be based on experience. Whether the result is theology, or spirituality, does not really matter. What matters is that I should try to talk about God in the way that I believe to be right.

Support from tradition

It is experience, confirmed by the principle of analogy, that has urged me to call God 'mother'. And yet, when I look at our Christian tradition — at those who have carried on the conversation before me — I find ample support for the notion of God's motherhood. Our tradition has indeed been very male-dominated, particularly in its understanding of God, but if we turn to many of the greatest spiritual writers we can find sufficient precedent for the imagery I have been using. We may not find anything about God's maternity in the great mass of minor theologians and preachers, but here and there among the really authoritative literature we find God compared to a mother, often with imagery that is quite physical even if it has not been as systematically developed as it is here. This is not the place for a detailed anthology, but some of the passages are so striking and beautiful that they are worth dwelling on.

Maternal imagery finds its way into the Old Testament, in both Psalms and Isaiah. Psalm 131, to take but one example, evokes the sense of security a child feels in the arms of its mother, in order to describe the peace we can feel with God:

> But I have calmed and quieted my soul,
> like a child quieted at its mother's breast;
> like a child that is quieted is my soul (Ps 131:2).

The repetitions ('quieted my soul . . . quieted . . . my soul', 'like a child . . . like a child') serve to emphasize the process of coming to rest and of letting worries and wonderings slip away. But it is not a sense of emptiness, but of rest *in a presence* — the presence of a mother, the presence of God. It is a sense I have been able often to observe in my own children, who find it very difficult to sit still and keep quiet, and are liable to try to monopolize attention if I have a visitor. But if they are able to sit on my knee and be cuddled they can enter quietly into that closeness and feel that nothing else is a threat to the attention they want. Bundles of energy that they are, they can become quite tranquil in my arms.

Isaiah uses a lot of imagery from motherhood to enrich language about God, but the most famous quotation is this:

> Can a woman forget her sucking child,
> > that she should have no compassion on the
> > son of her womb?
> Even these may forget,
> > yet I will not forget you (Is 49:15).

Often in the Old Testament, sin is spoken of under the image of forgetfulness. But even if we forget God, she will never forget us. The remembrance of a mother for her own child is here used as the most powerful instance imaginable of human fidelity. It is true that a mother cannot forget her breastfeeding baby. Every four hours, at least, there will be those little, persistent cries. And yet I have sometimes forgotten, for a little. I once got in the car with Dominic and Cordelia and drove two or three streets away, before remembering that the undemanding Benedict was fast asleep in his cot, alone in the house. But I cannot forget for long, because after a while my breasts tingle with overflowing milk, even if my conscious memory clock has failed to operate. God is more of a mother than any human mother can ever be. Even though she is doing a dozen other things at the same time there is not even an instant in which she forgets us.

In the New Testament, the author of 1 Peter extends the well-established imagery of new birth through Christ to suggest that as Christians we are babies, feeding on the milk of God's kindness:

> You have been born anew, not of perishable seed
> but of imperishable, through the living and
> abiding word of God . . . . Like newborn babes,
> long for the pure spiritual milk, that by it you
> may grow up to salvation; for you have tasted
> the kindness of the Lord (1 Pet 1:23 – 2:3).

We are well familiar with the idea of baptism as a new birth, but for most of us it all happened so long ago that it does not occur to us to think of ourselves as spiritual babies of God. But birth is not the end of the matter — on the contrary it is only just the beginning. Without care and nourishment we will fail to grow to adulthood, fail to 'grow up to salvation'. What better image for the care and nourishment we need than the mother's milk? It comes from the mother itself, it is given in love and kindness, it is sweet to the taste and the child longs for it. And so it is God herself who nourishes our spiritual growth, and she does so with love and kindness; spiritual sustenance is sweet to us, and we hunger for it.

The great Eastern Father, Gregory of Nyssa, gives us an appealing image of the way God communicates to us as a mother to her babies:

> The divine power . . . is like a mother,
> compassionate to the inarticulate whimperings
> of her infants, who joins in their burblings . . .
> (*Contra Eunomium*, 2; ed. W. Jaeger, 1,
> 348.22–26).

We have all heard mothers cooing and making inarticulate noises at their babies, to elicit either their smiles or their responding burbles, and those of us who are mothers know that in private we do this with far less restraint. Stupid as we feel if observed, we enjoy this communing on our babies' level, and it helps to build up our relationship with them. More than that, it teaches them language: slowly and imperceptibly they learn to use their voices as we use ours. It is amusing and reassuring to think of God doing the same with us — to think of her enjoying her nonsense talk with us, confident that we will learn through it her language. We need not be embarrassed by our childish concepts, because even our most learned abstractions are childish talk to God.

We can learn to enjoy talking to God — enjoy the nonsense of it, knowing she enjoys it too, and that through it she is teaching us more than we can yet dream of.

The best known of all the early Fathers, St Augustine, was one of the many authorities from our tradition to speak of God feeding us from her breast:

> Without you I am my own guide to the brink of perdition. And even when all is well with me, what am I but a creature suckled on your milk and feeding on yourself, the food that never perishes? (*Confessions*, IV.1; tr. R. S. Pine-Coffin, Penguin Books, Harmondsworth, 1961, p. 71).

When Augustine speaks of 'feeding on yourself' he probably has in mind the eucharist in particular as well as the general sustaining care of God. He draws attention to the fact that it is not just that God gives us our food, but that she is our food. At the same time I think he would wish to include every kind of milk of spiritual nourishment, sacramental or not. And this milk, because it springs straight from the body of the mother — straight from the person of God — is always fresh, unperishing. When we think of the complicated manoeuvres of sterilization used in the twentieth-century West to render bottle-milk safe for babies, we have a vivid reminder of the value of this imperishability. The nourishment God gives us is not subject to deterioration, because it is produced specially for us at just the moment we need it. The God who makes 'all things new' (Rev 21:5) also gives us all things new.

In the Middle Ages, St Anselm calls God explicitly by the title of 'mother'. He also calls St Paul a mother, in a derived sense, because he mediates to us the new birth brought by Christ:

> So you, Lord God, are the great mother.
> Then both of you are mothers.
> Even if you are fathers, you are also mothers.
> For you have brought it about that those born to death
> should be reborn to life —
> you by your own act, you by his power
> ('Prayer to St Paul', 415–420; *The Prayers and*

Meditations of St Anselm, tr. B. Ward, Penguin Books, Harmondsworth, 1973, p. 154).

Anselm is clear that the use of the image of fatherhood by no means excludes that of motherhood. On the contrary, motherhood is particularly apt for someone who has brought us to a new birth. Fathers beget, but they do not give birth — only a mother can give birth. In our new, spiritual birth — the birth of re-creation to eternal life — the mother must be God. 'So you, Lord God, are the great mother.' Anyone who has a ministry in bringing people to their second birth has a share in this motherhood. If St Paul can be called a mother, many other preachers too, men or women, must discover the maternal side of their ministry. If we learn to look at God in a new way — as our mother — we will also learn to look at our own responsibilities in a new way, enriched by the notion of bringing others to new birth and caring for them as a mother.

Perhaps the best known exponent of God's motherhood is the fourteenth-century female hermit, Julian of Norwich. She too draws on the idea that we are re-born through our divine mother, and feed on her milk in the eucharist, and she develops the theme in many other rich ways as well. In this passage she reflects on the way a troubled child seeks help and forgiveness from its mother:

> But often when our falling and our wretchedness are shown to us, we are so much afraid and so greatly ashamed of ourselves that we scarcely know where we can put ourselves. But then our courteous Mother does not wish us to flee away, for nothing would be less pleasing to him; but he then wants us to behave like a child. For when it is distressed and frightened, it runs quickly to its mother; and if it can do no more, it calls to the mother for help with all its might. So he wants us to act as a meek child saying: My kind Mother, my gracious Mother, my beloved Mother, have mercy on me. I have made myself filthy and unlike you, and I may not and cannot make it right except with your help and grace (*Showings* — Long Text, ch.61; tr. E. Colledge and J. K.

Walsh, Classics of Western Spirituality, Paulist Press, New York, 1978, p.301).

It is quite true that the only way out of distress for a child is to turn to its mother, and however stupid or disobedient it has been the mother always wants to receive it, because she knows there is no other way. I am reminded of one night when Cordelia woke with a nightmare. Peter and I in turn tried to comfort her, but she flailed around screaming 'No, go away, don't touch me, I don't want you'. If we went away, of course, she cried all the more. Then, after five or ten minutes, she suddenly quietened and came into my arms and said 'Sorry Mummy' and it was all over. I held her and kissed her and tucked her up to sleep again. There is no other way but to run to our mother's arms, even if for a while we want to run in the other direction and flail about on our own. Not only is our mother willing to receive us back, but she is standing there waiting for the first sign that we will allow ourselves to be helped.

Julian's Italian contemporary, Catherine of Siena, made occasional use of the breast-feeding analogy, as in this strikingly original passage:

> But when the great doctor came (my only-begotten Son) he tended that wound, drinking himself the bitter medicine you could not swallow. And he did as the wet nurse who herself drinks the medicine the baby needs, because she is big and strong and the baby is too weak to stand the bitterness. My son was your wet nurse, and he joined the bigness and strength of his divinity with your nature to drink the bitter medicine of his painful death on the cross so that he might heal and give life to you who were babies weakened by sin (*The Dialogue*, XIV; tr. S. Noffke, Classics of Western Spirituality, SPCK, London, 1980, p.52).

When Catherine speaks of the wet nurse, she could as easily speak of the mother: the point is that she is speaking of the woman who breast-feeds the baby. We have been accustomed to speaking of Christ as our redeemer — using a metaphor of someone buying the freedom of a slave. But here Catherine uses a metaphor that captures far more effectively two essential aspects of that 'redemption': firstly, there is the sense of substitution, in which Christ bears the suffering due to us; secondly, there is the sense of intimate communion with him, that enables us to draw the fruits of the salvation he has won. Though the practice of drinking a bitter medicine on behalf of the child is not current today we can easily see the sense of it, and there is something very beautiful and loving about the woman acting as mediator in this way. Not only do we find yet another richness in the concept of divine maternity, but the uneasy theological notion of substitution attains new meaning as we see it conjoined to the idea of loving communion — most particularly realized, of course, in the eucharist.

Breast-feeding figures again, frequently, in the writings of Teresa of Avila, the great Spanish Carmelite. She uses it as a picture of the soul at prayer. Speaking of the prayer of quiet she says:

> The soul is like an infant still at its mother's breast: such is the mother's care for it that she gives it its milk without its having to ask for it so much as by moving its lips. That is what happens here. The will simply loves, and no effort needs to be made by the understanding, for it is the Lord's pleasure that, without exercising its thought, the soul should realize that it is in His company, and should merely drink the milk which His Majesty puts into its mouth and enjoy its sweetness. The Lord desires it to know that it is He Who is granting it that favour and that in its enjoyment of it He too rejoices (*The Way of Perfection*, ch. XXXI; tr. Allison Peers, *The Complete Works of St Teresa of Jesus*, vol.2, Sheed and Ward, London, 1946, pp.130–131).

I find it very helpful to have prayer spoken of in this way. The one experience — that of feeding a child — is so deeply meaningful to me, despite its familiarity, that I am encouraged to be told that prayer is like that. At times when my prayer is dry I am reminded how worthwhile and consoling it will be if I persevere; at times when my prayer is sweet it is reassuring to have my experience confirmed as authentic. It is good to know that the sweetness of prayer is not something I create by my own efforts, but a relishing of a gift in utter receptivity: where perseverance is required, it is a concentration on relaxation and awareness, not a screwing up to great feats. It is good too (though here I hardly dare believe it) to know that in my times of prayerful consolation God is as happy to give the gift as I am to receive it.

The final quotation I would like to ponder comes from Angelo Roncalli, better known as Pope John XXIII, the Pope who 'opened the windows of the Vatican' and called the Second Vatican Council. While still a student at seminary, he wrote this entry in his diary about God's care for him:

> He took me, a country lad, from my home, and
> with the affection of a loving mother he has
> given me all I needed. I had nothing to eat and he
> provided food for me, I had nothing to wear and
> he clothed me, I had no books to study and he
> provided those also. At times I forgot him and he
> always gently recalled me. If my affection for
> him cooled, he warmed me in his breast, at the
> flame with which his Heart is always
> burning . . . and he still cares for me without
> respite, day and night, more than a mother cares
> for her child (10–20 December 1902; *Journal of
> a Soul*, tr. D. White, Geoffrey Chapman,
> London, rev. ed. 1980, pp.95–96).

It is interesting that despite the pressures of traditional thinking Roncalli should have chosen to use the image of the mother for God's care rather than that of father. Perhaps he felt more free to experiment because he was writing purely for his own eyes, in his private diary. Perhaps, too, it had been a fact of his own experience as a child that provision, affection and guidance had been more associated with his mother than with his father. Many people, if they look into their personal experience, would say the same.

This small collection of quotations gives some idea of what can be found in our tradition to support the image of God's motherhood. Many other passages can be found, both in these writers and in others like Meister Eckhart, St Bernard and St Francis de Sales to confirm and encourage a maternal vision of God. We may think of it as a minor part of our tradition, because generally it has escaped our notice. But once we stop and examine it, it proves full of riches.

There is, however, one important person in Christian tradition who does not talk of God as a mother — Jesus himself. Jesus likens himself at one point to a mother hen: 'How often would I have gathered your children together as a hen gathers her brood under her wings, and you would not!' (Mt 23:37; Lk 13:34). But when he teaches about God it is a 'father' he speaks of, and not a mother or unspecified parent. This relationship to his 'father', whom he calls by the familiar term of 'Abba', lies at the heart of Jesus' understanding of God and even provides the keynote of the religious language that is distinctively personal to him.

Of all the models for God that could be used — 'judge', 'teacher', 'healer' and so on — none is closer to that of 'mother' than 'father' is. Why did Jesus' strong sense of the fatherhood of God not lead him that small extra step, to the discovery of God's motherhood? One might have expected the occasional maternal simile to slip in, even if he did not take the step of actually calling God 'mother'. There was, after all, precedent for this in some passages of the Old Testament, as we have seen. Why should Jesus stick so rigidly to the male model?

We can only guess at an answer, but here is one suggestion. If there was indeed some question mark hanging over his parentage, Jesus may have needed to find a father in heaven because he did not feel he had a proper father on earth. He already had an adequate mother in Mary, and did not feel the need to supplement her with a heavenly mother. But Joseph — however good a foster-parent he was — could never fill the father role completely. It would have been natural for Jesus to look to God to fulfil what was left unsatisfied in human terms — in this case, a father–son relationship.

Further to this, Jesus' work was not to carry on Joseph's trade of carpentry. No, his work was God's work, and in John's gospel he sometimes speaks of himself almost as God's apprentice: 'Truly, truly, I say to you, the Son can do nothing of his own accord, but only what he sees the Father doing; for whatever he does, that the Son does likewise' (Jn 5:19). In a society where it was the norm to carry on the work done by the parent of the same sex, it could be expected that a male Jesus, carrying on the work of God, would feel he was following a Father rather than a Mother. Jesus, I suggest, thought of God as male because he himself was male.

Whether this suggestion is acceptable or not, Jesus' own male language for God need not stop us extending what he says in legitimate ways. We will not go back on what Jesus taught us — on the contrary, we find it opens up new vistas. One of these vistas may be to find God as a mother. Without actually saying 'God is our mother' there is no closer preparation for it than saying 'God is our father'. If we find the motherhood of God means something to us, we are justified in talking in those terms precisely because Jesus did call God 'father'.

Which model we prefer will depend on who we are: it will depend on what experiences we have had and what experiences we feel we need. People who have had a mother but never been a mother may, like Jesus, be affected less by this type of language: it may simply speak less to them. On the other hand, sometimes these are precisely the people most in need of a mother God, just as it is sometimes celibate clergy who are most dependent on devotion to Mary as mother. And at the other end of the scale, those for whom mothering has been the most important event in their lives will have a great need to bring this experience into the heart of their way of relating to God.

The propriety of the 'mother' or the 'father' model will also depend very largely on context. It may be more natural, for example, to call God 'father' when we are relating to him quite consciously through the mediation of Christ. If we are recalling the work of Jesus as our forerunner, we expect to pick up and copy Jesus' own terminology, and that includes his use of the term 'father', or 'Abba'. 'God sent forth his Son . . . so that we might receive adoption as sons. And because you are sons, God has sent the Spirit of his Son into our hearts, crying, "Abba! Father!" (Gal 4:4–6).

But when the stress falls more on the creative and protective powers of God, we may find 'mother' language more expressive, for all the reasons of which I have spoken throughout this book. It is a mother who carried us safely in her womb; it is a mother who brings us to birth; it is a mother who gives us our first nourishment. It is this relationship with a mother that enables all other relationships to be formed; it is this relationship that is chronologically and psychologically prior; it is this relationship, therefore, that is privileged as the model for the God who creates us, cherishes us, nourishes us and bestows on us the gift of love. We cannot but accept that God is our mother.

Add to that the Christological aspects of God's motherhood that our tradition has brought before our eyes: that in Christ we are re-born . . . that in feeding on the body of Christ we are feeding on God herself . . . . Then we see that our mother God belongs not only to creation but to new creation, not only to monotheism but to Christianity.

17

Postlude:
handing on the faith

I said in my introduction that this is an unusual book. It has not been a typical autobiographical account of having children — there has been too much reflective and theological material for that. Nor has it been a straight theological work — there has been too much personal story for that. So what in the end have I wanted to write about? Motherhood? Or God?

Put blankly like that, the falseness of the question comes across. Do we want to go on keeping God isolated from the rest of life, in the way we have done for so many centuries, and that has contributed so much to the decline of Christianity in the Western world? If we do, then this book is an absurdity: it disrupts our division; it breaks the rules.

Or do we want to find God in all things? To illumine our religion with our life, and our life with our religion? To discover new depths and breadths to our spiritual life, not by withdrawing from what the world can offer, but by letting the awareness of God stream into — and out of — the furthest corners of experience? That has been my aim, and that has been the point of this book.

But such a thorough-going attempt as I have made has to be something of an experiment. Despite the only too apparent reasons for trying to write wholly about motherhood and wholly about God and both at the same time, the result may still feel to some people a little uncomfortable. Is that a fault on the part of the book or is it due to habit? Is my attempt at a thoroughly experience-based theology, and a thoroughly God-based account of motherhood, in the end jagged and unworkable? Or are we so secure in the limited God we have that we want to resist the invitation to find her in new places and new language? Maybe there is a little of both, but only time can tell, and only then if the experiment is made, if the book is written, if the risk is taken.

In the end what I have wanted to write about is God, and I have wanted to write about motherhood as a way into writing about God. Suppose I took out of this book all the bits of personal experience, and left the God-bits on their own: would they mean as much? If so, this book is a failure. But if what I have to say about God gains force and richness, in however small a way, from being spoken out of the depths of common human experience, then I will feel I have achieved my aim. I shall be satisfied if I have helped anyone to find a God who is even a fraction more real, more loving, more warm. There is no point at all in calling God our mother, unless it can lead to that.

But then it is also true that in the end what I have wanted to write about is motherhood, and I have wanted to write about God as a way — the only way — to find the full, true meaning of motherhood. I have written, not for Christians first, nor for mothers first, but for both groups, in the belief that a deeper understanding of God is at the same time a deeper understanding of humanity, and a deeper understanding of humanity is at the same time a deeper understanding of God.

With that reminder of what this book is trying to do, it is time to end where I began, with the teaching of children. In the prelude I recalled how my mother and the Mothers tried to give me a knowledge of God; now in this concluding chapter I recount my own attempts as a mother with my own children. There would be little point in finding God in our own experience of motherhood if we were not to go on from there to spread the word, to hand on the faith, and to help others to find the God who is our mother.

*

Handing on the Christian faith is one of the greatest privileges of a mother. I do it with joy and fear. Joy, because although I may never make any converts I can at least bring new people into the Church as children. I can see them baptized, even plan their baptisms. I can supervise exactly what they learn about God in their earliest years, choosing the words for their very first lessons about God, hoping to plant good seed in good earth. Fear, because it is actually extremely difficult to do well, and I even feel I am drawing on my entire theological education to formulate the simplest truth. The more condensed you must be, the more discerning you must be. Some of my mistakes and difficulties I can see as I go along, others perhaps will trouble me as my children grow up and 'lose their faith'. There is no handbook for explaining Christian beliefs to children under five, and even if there was I would no doubt find fault with it. But though I have this thin layer of hesitation I am comforted by the knowledge that it is not just permissible but obligatory for me to try. I may have to be cautious about preaching the faith to adults or to other people's children, but when it comes to my own it is my responsibility and I may not draw back.

Much of the education is non-verbal. We go every Sunday to church. We have pictures of the children's saints over their beds. They see me slipping off to weekday mass from time to time, or silently sitting in my prayer-hole. They have little silver crosses to put round their necks when they feel like it, and they know the cross is what Jesus died on. At Christmas there are cribs; at Easter there is a model I made out of papier-mâché of a hill with three crosses on the top and an empty tomb at the foot. They hear endlessly, through Peter's work, of the Pope, and have been personally touched and blessed by him when we lived in Rome. They know, through us, many priests, and they know how a priest is the one who stands in front and says the words for a mass. They came and saw our little Benedict baptized — an event of such importance that we woke them up in the middle of the night for it. They are not, I must admit, children of great piety, but at least they know something pretty major is going on.

When it comes to actually talking about the faith, my teaching has focused on two main areas. I speak to them about God as the one who made everything, can do anything, and loves and looks after us. Then I speak to them about Jesus, whose mummy was Mary and whose birthday is Christmas, who was killed on a cross by soldiers and came to life again at Easter. When I talk to them about these things, it is nearly always at bedtime: that is the time when we have a story — which is on occasion religious — and a song to Jesus. After the hymn, if they are in a receptive mood — which very often they are not — I pray with them and tell them about God or about Jesus.

This prompted Dominic to ask, very early on, one of the most difficult questions I could imagine: 'Is Jesus God?' I swallowed, and said 'Yes', adding, as a nuance that I knew would be incomprehensible but I hoped would give the idea that it was not quite as simple as that: 'He is the Son of God. He is a man, he was in the world like us, but he was totally open to God's Spirit — not like us — and now he lives in heaven with God.' As I burbled on in my foreign language I began to feel the less said the better. However, all the children picked up was the positive answer 'Yes', and now they swop attributes indiscriminately, talking of Jesus as the one who made us, and God as the one on the cross, to which I reply 'Yes, God made us', or 'Yes, Jesus was on the cross', reassuring myself with the classical doctrine that whatever can be affirmed of one member of the Trinity can also be affirmed of the others, with accuracy if not with aptness.

Another thing I have found difficult to explain is the non-bodily presence of Jesus. When asked, in the *present* tense, 'Has Jesus got a beard?' I found it difficult to know if the correct answer should be 'Yes'. When asked 'Will Jesus come on the plane with us to England?' I of course said 'Yes' because of his continual presence, but Dominic then asked 'Where will he sit?' 'He does not need a seat', I said, 'because he will not be with us with his body' (I was careful not to say 'He has not got a body'), but Dominic said 'What's a body?' and after a careful if somewhat lengthy attempt to explain what a body was (as opposed to a 'soul' or 'spirit' — ha! ha! tricky waters, what would the Oxford Professor of Moral and Pastoral Theology say?) Dominic looked completely unconvinced and finished the conversation decisively with 'Well, he will have to sit on my knee'.

Nonetheless one makes slow and somewhat charming progress, and by the age of four-and-a-half Dominic was informing me 'There are two ways of getting strong. One is by eating spinach, and the other is by Jesus making you strong', thus raising philosophical questions of the nature of divine activity that I thought it unnecessary to go into at

this stage. By the age of five-and-a-half Dominic was im-
provising a little song:

> Jesus is strong.
> Jesus can smash houses in two seconds.
> Jesus can fly.
> Jesus is just like Popeye,
> only stronger.

If I can develop a theology of motherhood according to
what is meaningful to me, I do not see why Dominic should
not develop a Popeye theology, according to what is meaningful to him.

But the difficulties I tried to meet in explaining the relationship of Father to Son, or the nature of non-bodily
presence, or the questions I tried to elude concerning the
mode of divine activity or the legitimacy of analogies from
personal experience, were as nothing compared to the
problems we ran into over the Passion and Resurrection.
When Dominic was three we followed the story with the
help of the little picture windows of a Lent calendar (like an
Advent Calendar, but no longer available: this one came
from my childhood). As we came to each character I placed
him on a scale of goodness or badness. Jesus is good, better
than anyone else in the whole world; his friends are good,
except that Peter was a bit bad when he said Jesus was not
his friend; Judas is quite a lot bad; the soldiers are bad (this
got established very early and rather unchangeably and I
cannot remember how), but not *very* bad because they
were doing what they were told (according to the criteria
for Dominic's own behaviour that should have made them
very good, but luckily I was not challenged on that point);
most bad are the chief priests, because they told the soldiers
to kill Jesus (this inaccuracy slipped in because it was quite
impossible to describe the intricacy of the different trials
and Temple–state relations). The line-up I ended up with
was not dissimilar to that of Thomas Aquinas as he answers
'Did those who crucified Christ commit the most grievous
of sins?' (*Summa Theologica,* III, q.47).

So far, so good, until Dominic announced one day to a
kind middle-aged friend, recently widowed, whose
husband had been in the army all his life: 'Soldiers are bad'.

'Oh, I do not think they all are, Dominic', she said, 'Why do you say that?' 'Because they killed Jesus', he replied. But a few months later he had acquired a taste for violence himself, and now said 'When I grow up I am going to be a soldier, and knock down those bad soldiers who killed Jesus with my sword'.

Resurrection faith I articulated in different ways at different ages. When Dominic was two I told him 'Jesus gets better'. By the age of four we had graduated to 'Jesus rose from the dead, and is alive now for always and always'. At the age of five I fed in — without further comment — 'and now lives with new life'. But Dominic's resurrection faith was so strong so early that I soon found we were having great difficulties with the notion of death.

When Dominic was three one of his favourite adult friends died. I gave him the news when he came in, and he said nonchalantly 'Oh, when will she get better?' I said that she would not, that she was dead and would always be dead now. He began to look suspicious. 'Where is she then?' he asked. I said she was in heaven with Jesus. He looked at me accusingly and tears began to form in his eyes. 'You said Jesus is dead. He's not dead, he's alive. You're wrong.' 'No I didn't.' 'Yes, you said she is with Jesus and she won't come alive any more. But Jesus is alive, not dead.'

I began to realize Dominic had a point — I am not at all clear about resurrection. It is easy enough to talk on one level — the ordinary, empirical level — about death being final. It is easy enough also to talk on another level — the level of accepted religious formulae — about dying and rising with Christ. The problem begins when you have to explain religious faith in ordinary empirical language, as you must do to a child. If 'rising with Christ' cannot be cashed in any way empirically at any time it ends up being meaningless. On the other hand too concrete and detailed an understanding of resurrection could be presumptuous and simplistic.

What exactly do we mean by saying we will have eternal life, and Christ will raise us up at the last day? Is it right to talk of the dead enjoying eternal life before that last day? And if so how do we answer a child's question 'Is she dead or alive?' Somehow we have to find words for our children that express the strength of our resurrection belief without giving the impression that we know exactly what it means.

Paul has just such a problem writing to the Corinthians about the nature of our risen bodies (1 Cor 15:35–57). At times he falls back on technical religious terms like 'physical body/spiritual body' that make us wonder exactly what a 'spiritual body' is like; at other times he is forced into empirical language that can only be meant metaphorically — 'the trumpet will sound'. But he manages to communicate something very rich despite the inevitable fumblings. It is magnificent poetry, but it is a lot more than that. He is talking about reality, and he means to be taken very seriously.

We too will fumble with our children, and frankly I am very glad to have a few well-known, over-simplified ideas to fall back on like going up into heaven and last trumpets sounding. But what we have to accept is that the reason we do not explain it very well is that we do not understand it very well, and what we are not understanding very well is something much more fundamental than the details of risen bodies. We have not quite discovered in our own lives what place this belief takes — when to mourn over death and when to rejoice over it for example; or when to make prudent choices for security in this world, and when to throw all caution away for the sake of the kingdom of heaven. Perhaps the need to explain it to our children will help us to face these problems more honestly, and to uncover the confusions in our understanding and in our values.

Along with these hesitations and stumblings there is great reward to be found in seeing my children understand a little bit more, year by year. I like to think that as I live through each liturgical year I myself progress, as first one aspect, then another, of the Christian mysteries unfolds and comes to the fore. When my children learn, they too in their childish way are joining on that path of understanding that goes on through the years. And when my time is past they too, I hope, will be handing on, so that through all the Christian centuries a long chain stretches, from mother to child, from mother to child, along which we all move and to the end of which we never come, until all understanding is made whole and balanced and perfect in the life to come.

*

I began this book with my mother, handing on the faith to me; now, as I hand on to my own children, I bring the story to an end. But all I have written has been an attempt to hand on, even if what I am handing on is not so much a received doctrine as a lived experience and the meaning that I have found in it. It will be evident that much of what I have spoken about is very personal to me, but I have done so in the hope that through all the particularities a message will be found that is universal. My God, and the God of Dominic, Cordelia and Benedict, is the one God to whom we all pray; and the truth of her love, discovered in all the exhilarating and frustrating details of my motherhood, is a truth that can be found by everyone, mother or not, female or not, because God's love is truth and it is a love for all. If this book has been able to evoke a sense of motherhood in those who read it, whether through their memories, their longings, or their sympathies, it will be because we are all made in the image of one mother and all have learnt from her, consciously or unconsciously, what it means to be gentle and caring, what it means to enfold and cherish, what it means to nourish and console. All comfort that comes from us, all creativity that breaks out from us, all tenderness that flows from us, comes ultimately from one source — our one, true and eternal mother, who is our God.